FAVERSHAM

IN OLD PHOTOGRAPHS

COURT STREET. Although reproduced elsewhere (see introduction) this early picture, taken in 1852, can hardly be omitted from any photographic record of Faversham since it is the earliest-known photograph of the town. Many of the buildings survive today despite the demolition of some to make way for new roads on both the right and left of the picture. The identity of the individuals making up the group is unknown, although the right-hand figure may quite possibly be Henry Shepherd, Sen. (1780–1862) who carried on the business of brewing at what is now Shepherd Neame. Henry Shepherd consistently wore knee breeches, which at the time this photograph was taken were distinctly out of fashion and belonged more properly to the eighteenth century. There is the probability that the worthy brewer, a prominent member of the town's community, would have posed with other like gentlemen of the town for the purpose of this photograph. Tantalizingly, it will probably never be proven one way or the other.

FAVERSHAM
IN OLD PHOTOGRAPHS

COLLECTED BY

ERIC R. SWAIN

ALAN SUTTON
1989

Alan Sutton Publishing Limited
Brunswick Road · Gloucester

First published 1989

British Library Cataloguing in Publication Data

Faversham in old photographs.

1. Kent. Faversham, history
I. Swain, Eric R.
942.2′33

ISBN 0-86299-544-2

Typesetting and origination by
Alan Sutton Publishing Limited.
Printed in Great Britain
by Dotesios Printers Limited.

CONTENTS

INTRODUCTION

The title of this book, *Faversham in Old Photographs* is necessarily succinct, but should be taken in its broader sense to mean Faversham and district. No English country town can be considered in isolation from the surrounding countryside, any more than the latter can be divorced in a historical context from the local market town. It is not the intention of this series to ignore this inter-relationship between town and country, indeed any historical study demonstrates that the one has always served, and partly depended upon, the other. Thus the 211 pictures in this book present an overall view of life in the town and surrounding countryside, using the Swale to the north as a natural boundary line, and reaching arbitrarily to Graveney, Boughton, Eastling, Newnham and Teynham on the east, south and west.

The geographic spread of the area included in the book does not mean that I have sought to represent every locality with one or more illustrations. Such an approach would have been doomed, for the availability of material, while perhaps almost embarrassingly plentiful for one area, may well be almost non-existent for another. Since the intention is to illustrate the lifestyle of the past 100 years plus in the area, a thematic approach has been adopted. Thus, to present a picture of 'Country Life and Work' for example, it matters little if one village is represented by far more photographs than is the case elsewhere, if the former collection of pictures is a good representation of country life and work within the overall area under review.

The town of Faversham has developed from an early settlement at the head of a tidal creek. That this occupation did not extend as far south as the survey line of the Roman road built from Dover to London seems fortuitous, because the road alignment later became used for the A2; undoubtedly the town would, over the years, have become a comparatively characterless place if it had been dissected by the trunk road to the coast. Instead, Faversham grew as an entity with a distinct nature of its own, formed from the proximity of creek and sea trade, royal favour, abbey, marsh and sheep, farming and fruit, gunpowder, brewing and bricks.

The Romans built their posting-station on Judd Folly Hill to the south-west of the town, with a temple nearby. They must have found the link with the sea via the creeks to be both useful and pleasant, for a villa was built near the settlement at the head of Faversham creek. After the departure of the Romans their road continued to be used, and the temple at Stone was also utilized by the converts of St Augustine, who followed his edict and put to Christian use this relic of a former heathen religion. Unfortunately it eventually became a victim of hard times and now stands forlorn in an empty field, maintained only by the edict of officialdom instead of the conviction of faith.

Faversham itself was favoured sufficiently by the Saxon kings of Kent to acquire the apellation of 'the king's town', quite probably being regarded as their capital. The town can still use the Royal Arms and the avaricious Normans were pleased to find a thriving town and port. It is frustrating that we can visualize so little of what it must have been like in Saxon Faversham, although many burial remains have been found with associated artefacts of fine quality. This association of the Saxon kings with the town has been kept alive by the use of their names for streets built at the beginning of this century. The practice has happily been continued in one area where property conversion and development has recently taken place.

Faversham Abbey, of which little trace now remains, was founded by King Stephen who was buried there with his queen. The town was known and visited by King Henry VIII, the Emperor Charles V on his visit to England, the half-sister queens, Elizabeth and Mary, and Charles II on his triumphal return to end the interregnum. Charles' brother James II had less reason to remember the town with affection. While he was attempting an unobtrusive exit from the country with the connivance of the government, Faversham sailors, with scant regard of such finer points of statesmanship, apprehended the unfortunate James on the Swale, hauled him into town with rough handling and locked him up. Imagine the hours of yarning in the town's plentiful ale houses that must have followed that local diversion. Shakespeare and Marlowe knew Faversham also, enough for one of them (or some like person of commendable talent) to have penned a play based on the murder in 1551 of poor Thomas Arden, former mayor of Faversham, with a true-life background plot of conspiracy and sexual intrigue involving Mrs Arden as the main villainess.

Commercial and trading concerns around the creek, together with two long-established breweries that continue to flourish, have combined with the success of surrounding agricultural interests to ensure that Faversham retains a characterful identity. An enormous number of medieval and later buildings survive in spite of the occasional hiccup in planning control, or even the odd collapse of official responsibility in passing some heavy-pressured 'development' (better called destruction), as for example in the case of some of the present shops at the lower end of Preston Street. Even so, the marvellous length of Court Street and Abbey Street, leading from the heart of the town to the site of the former abbey, remains lined with a wonderful array of period buildings scarcely equalled elsewhere in their variety and degree of preservation.

There has been a long-felt need for the publication of a meaningful and representative survey of Faversham and the life of its inhabitants over the past 100 years plus through the medium of photographs. While this book was in preparation, Mr Arthur Percival brought out his excellent work entitled *Old Faversham* and, although there are of course the several subject titles which have been published by the Faversham Society, they are not generally illustrated since the method of printing is unsuitable. Such is the amount of surviving photographic evidence that only a relatively small number of the illustrations that follow in this book have been reproduced together elsewhere. The scope of the present work is also wide enough to include a picture of rural life in the surrounding area, partly self-supportive, and partly supportive of the economy of Faversham, with which there was a certain interdependence. Unfortunately no one ever set out to make a comprehensive pictorial record of life in the area at any one time, still less over a long period, although it is due to the unflagging efforts of some local photographers, W. Hargrave and Theo Barber among them, that there exists such rewarding records. Inevitably there are gaps, not only geographically but in subject matter. Perhaps publications such as this will prompt the discovery or release of further collections that undoubtedly exist, and lead to further opportunities to marvel at past scenes.

The method of presentation in the book has been to group pictures thematically under general subject headings. Some overlap will always occur with this method, e.g. a procession with a background of interesting buildings in a prominent street could perhaps be included under either 'Events, celebrations, etc.' or equally well in the section headed 'Town and Buildings'. In such cases arbitrary decisions have to be made, and wherever it has been thought useful to the reader, references to other pages have been made in the captions. The extensive source material available, already alluded to above, is partly the result of the 'golden age' of postcard production from about 1900 to the First World War, when many cards were produced from photographs of scenes and events of the period. A perverse consequence of the decline in popularity of such postcards is the comparative scarcity of photographs illustrating local life and times of later periods, e.g. the Second World War. The largest single source is probably that of the local newspapers, but in my enquiries very little evidence of this period materialized in private collections. It will not be long before the end of that particular conflict attains its fiftieth anniversary; now would be a very good time to start preparation of an illustrated work encompassing the living memories of some who experienced the war locally. The memories of yesterday are indeed the stuff of history.

Finally, no dedication is needed for such a publication as this other than to the people of Faversham themselves. It belongs to them; without their contributions it could not have been produced and proper acknowledgement is made at the end of the book.

SECTION ONE

Town and Buildings

AT THE TURN OF THE CENTURY, postcards were entering a golden age of popularity and a typical type, which is produced to this day, was the composite group of views such as that shown here. Ideal for sale to the visitor to the town, this postcard shows the Recreation Ground and Bandstand with church spire in the distance, the Guildhall (here called the Town Hall), the Parish Church of St Mary of Charity, The Mall complete with the horse trough that is now used for growing flowers and the Creek with busy wharfside.

THE GUILDHALL in Market Place is probably the best known view of Faversham. The pillars and arcading remain from the 1574 court hall; the upper part is an elegant early nineteenth-century rebuild following a fire. The opportunity was taken to extend the building to the north and it is still used by the town council. There is within a list of all the town mayors from the thirteenth century onwards (see pages 12 & 87 bottom).

THE ENTRANCE TO THE MALL on a summer's day *c.* 1905. The intention of providing an impressive approach to the town as envisaged in the late eighteenth century was partly negated some eighty years later when the railway required the building of a level crossing across the upper end of Preston Street. Despite this the continuation of the road via The Mall to the London thoroughfare still provided a direct link to the town centre. However the closing of the railway crossing in 1897 and diversion of road traffic, via a new road loop and underpass, has resulted in a devious route that belies the first impressions of The Mall approach. This photograph shows the attractive junction with the present A2, a scene that has not greatly changed.

MARKET PLACE, c. 1914. A splendid vintage motor-bus stands before the Guildhall. The eye is led down Court Street and to the right stands the corner buiding which, before the addition of the plain Georgian façade seen here, displayed the sixteenth-century timber-framing of a town house not greatly dissimilar to the present 1920s building erected with pseudo-timbering (see below and pages 11 top & 87 bottom).

THE GUILDHALL around 1930 with awnings shielding some of the stalls of market traders beneath the arcading. On the right is the building erected in the 1920s and referred to above. The shop windows further down Court Street were almost all protected from the sun by awnings, some of which were supported on poles slotted into pavement sockets. (See also pages 11 top & 87 bottom.)

THE UPPER END OF WEST STREET in *c.* 1900 showing well-stocked shop windows and outside displays of merchandise. Down the hill on the left can be seen the twin gable ends of the Sun Inn, dating from the fifteenth century with later additions. On the right-hand side, the second shop in the photograph, with two first-floor bay windows, has for many years been known as 'Gullivers'. The front is pargetted with moulded and decorated plasterwork including the date 1697.

A LOWER PART OF WEST STREET, c. 1910, showing that although not every building remains, many may still be identified with the existing premises. The entry to North Lane, nowadays much widened and aligned with South Road, may be seen halfway down the slope on the right. The White Horse is the second building on the further corner (see facing page). On the left where the road bends are the arched windows of number 20 where the solicitors Tassell & Son have been in occupation since 1848. Many of the foreground buildings have a structural basis in the fifteenth and sixteenth centuries.

WEST STREET retains an astonishing number of centuries-old buildings, particularly in the upper end leading to Market Place. The lower end nearer the creek was the oldest part of the town. This view of *c.* 1913 is looking east towards the North Lane/South Road crossroads. On the left is the White Horse; the next building abutting it was demolished to facilitate the widening of North Lane.

COURT STREET, looking north from Market Place in the early 1900s over part of the earlier market site, which is now once more used for the same purpose. Relatively little change has taken place in the vista of building façades stretching away into Abbey Street to the north, comprising a unique collection of medieval and later period buildings. Part of the foreground road has now been restored to its earlier surface of granite setts, and the street market is held there on certain weekdays (see page 27).

THE JUNCTION OF THE A2 AND THE ASHFORD ROAD seen in around 1907. Whether out for a walk with the pram or driving a horse and trap along the A2, there was time 'to stand and stare'. The large house in the background was Alfred House, home of Mr and Mrs Harry Neame. Mr Neame was the managing director of brewers Shepherd Neame for many years and was responsible for much development and expansion in the brewery. Alfred House has now been replaced by modern houses and the only identifiable features of the scene that may still be found are the roadside bank on the far left, the left-hand brick pier of the gateway seen on the left and the cedar tree in the centre of the picture, which now stands taller although it has lost many boughs.

THE SOUTH SIDE OF THE OLD LEVEL CROSSING IN PRESTON STREET showing a Georgian-fronted house, a jettied timber-framed building of probably late sixteenth-century date and, nearest the camera, the old forge. These buildings were demolished at the end of the nineteenth century when the railway station was rebuilt and extended. The continuation of Preston Street on the north side of the gates can be discerned on the left of the picture (see pages 74, 75 & 76).

PRESTON STREET FORGE at the end of the nineteenth century, showing a group of farriers and smiths outside the forge referred to on page 17. The site is now level and occupied by part of the railway station car park, which is fronted by the remnant of Preston Street connected only to the main northern part by the pedestrian tunnel under the railway.

PRESTON STREET as depicted on a postcard used in 1906. The well-known clock on the extreme left still overhangs the street as did the 'Gatefield House tree' on the right, although this has long since disappeared. Edwardian costumes and a fine summer's day combined with attractive shop façades to make this very pleasant picture.

PRESTON STREET from the top (south) end, with the railings and gateway lamp of the Methodist church on the extreme right. Just beyond was Barton's 'Hair Cutting and Shaving Saloon' in a seventeenth-century house of Dutch influence, although the gable has been much mutilated. Pictured in around 1912, the only traffic was either horse- or hand-drawn, plus one or two bicycles. In the distance can be seen the tall chimney at Rigden's brewery (now Whitbread's).

PRESTON, looking across the main Canterbury road towards the present allotments and council yard at around the beginning of this century. Some children have paused from playing with their hoops, and other people are engaged in leisurely conversation. Although a street lamp and footpath with kerb was provided on one side of the road, the nearside with open drain and rough path merging into the gravelly roadway presents a revealing glimpse of the main route from London to Dover at that time.

THE APPEARANCE OF THE A2 THROUGH OSPRINGE around 1910 was not so greatly unlike that of today. Although normally subjected to heavy bombardment from traffic, there are still occasions such as an early weekend morning when a clear road like this may be glimpsed. Although each building remains, the Lion Inn and The Mayor's Arms have both ceased to trade as public houses.

THIS HEAVILY-LADEN CART stood in the mucky kerbside in Ospringe Street in 1905. On the right of the cart can be seen the jettied overhand of the two wings of the 'Wealden' hallhouse, which still exists next to the Anchor Inn, sporting an attractive gas lamp on the pillared porch. Further down the street on the left stands the Ship Inn on the corner of Ospringe Road. These licensed premises are the only two remaining in this short street where once five pubs tempted thirsty travellers and locals alike.

OSPRINGE STREET looking west. On the right-hand corner is the Ship Inn advertising good beds and stabling. The large tree has gone, but the wall survives with the difference that it now bears evidence of later, more worrying times. In the Second World War it was pierced with loopholes for guns, thus providing a potential position of defence against any possible invader approaching down the main road from Canterbury. Although the embrasures may still be seen today their effectiveness was thankfully never tested.

SYNDALE. Formerly standing to the south of the present A2, above the Newnham road, this seventeenth-century mansion was destroyed by a fire in 1961. The house had been built by Daniel Judd, a successful operator in the Faversham gunpowder industry. However, his enthusiastic support of the Parliamentarian cause did not go unremarked after the restoration of the monarchy in 1660 and the unfortunate Judd lost his mansion. The hill is still called 'Judd Folly Hill'. Some part of the former outbuildings remain on the site which now incorporates a motel.

OSPRINGE ROAD, FAVERSHAM, c. 1915. Traffic still presented no great hazard to judge by the children watching the photographer. The Faversham Arms on the left partly occupies a site which was known as Hangman's Field as far back as 1686, and later referred to as Gallows Hole Field. The public house was built in around 1850 and the occupier at the time of this photograph was probably Jesse Pilcher.

DAVINGTON PRIORY. The remains of the Benedictine nunnery still remain and the tower is the survivor of a former twelfth-century pair (cf. Reculver near Herne Bay). The nuns seemed always to lead a problematical life, their foundation lasted from its inception in 1153 to about 1536, when they quite literally died out at this site. An eighteenth-century engraving shows two further gables to the right of the four seen here, but they were apparently demolished in 1781.

THE PRESENT PRIVATELY-OWNED PRIORY abutting the church (used for parish worship) comprises some of the former priory cloisters. There is much of historical interest including survivals of the work of Thomas Willement who exercised his considerable, and nationally-important, skills in painting and stained-glass production in the restoration of priory and church in the late nineteenth century.

FAVERSHAM ALMS HOUSES, c. 1900, illustrating some of the fine Victorian features of this splendid group of buildings. In latter years a private bequest has aided extensive restoration. The complex of dwellings and chapel was built in 1863 by the architects Hooker and Wheeler, with a Thomas Willement west window transferred from the parish church earlier this century.

EAST STREET in 1909 looking towards the town centre. Church Road is on the right and opposite Cooksditch (see page 26 top) which is just out of sight on the right, a uniformed chauffeur waits next to one of the earliest motor cars in the town. In the right-hand middle of the picture is the Recreation Tavern with jettied first floor overhanging the street. At one time this public house was owned by Rigdens and their successors. Mabel Beane became the licensed tenant in 1933 and remained there for 28 years, the house being popularly called after her. The name Recreation Tavern dates only from some time after 1860 when the recreation ground was laid out. The building is much older than that, demonstrably sixteenth-century or earlier, and must have been built on what was the outer edge of town at that time. (See page 28 top).

COOKSDITCH IN EAST STREET, on the corner of Church Road, occupies the site of an earlier house and was built by Stephen Gillow before 1790. His widow Elizabeth added the splendid one-storey wings by 1798, complementing the elegant Ionic stone porch of the main building. The whole is now used as a private home for older citizens. It is one of the most impressive houses in Faversham and is pictured here in around 1914.

COURT STREET in *c.* 1909 with the proud flag flying above Child's department store. On the left can be seen the rows of lights outside the shop fronts to illuminate the extensive displays of goods on dark evenings. The wide road attests to its former use as an open market, which latterly has been reintroduced. The dirty-looking thoroughfare leads down to Abbey Street in the distance and behind the tall building on the near right hand is the northern access to Middle Row (see page 15 bottom).

Bottom left.

THE STRIKINGLY IMPOSING CONGREGATIONAL CHURCH in Newton Road (now the site of Herbert Dane Court) contrasted strongly with most of the architecture in Faversham. No longer able to be supported by its dwindling congregation, it was sold and demolished in 1975, just 96 years after it was built. It was undoubtedly a loss to the town, with a splendid interior that could and should have been utilized for community use. Regrettably Faversham was not ready to appreciate it.

EAST STREET, c. 1930. In this picture it is possible to identify existing buildings and thus pinpoint those lost. On the left can be seen the large Faversham Institute building, demolished in 1979 and now replaced by John Anderson Court. Further on, beyond the opening of Newton Road, are older structures including the three gables and jettied overhang of a sixteenth-century timber-framed house where a post office and supermarket are now sited. Almost opposite, further demolition has taken place to allow Crescent Road to form a link into Court Street, and the horse and cart stand outside The Recreation Tavern (see page 25).

FAVERSHAM CATTLE MARKET was situated roughly where the central car park is now. Back Lane, adjacent to Curling's butcher's shop and sometimes called Curling's Alley (see p. 89) led from Market Street to the market which is seen in this photograph in the late 1920s. The name board displayed on the left is that of Cooper Heyman, Auctioneer & Valuer. Local butchers bought livestock at the market, competing for prize beasts at the fatstock show before Christmas and using the prize certificates and rosettes to embellish their shop displays.

SECTION TWO

Creeks and Commerce

A FINE PICTURE OF T.G. GILLETT'S MILL AND WHARF, *c.* 1906, on Faversham Creek. The imposing centre building, overlooking the sailing barges moored along the wharf, is still in use today by Gillett's, who remain prominent among the creekside businesses. The creek was improved for navigation in the 1840s with new channels being cut to straighten some of the worst meanderings of the water course. Small vessels still use the facilities which have survived the competition of other local harbours. Agricultural feedstuffs, fertilizer and timber are among the goods handled here. In this old picture the creek is seen at high tide – undeniably more attractive than when the mud is exposed. Sluice gates just above this point are used to flush out the influx of sedimentary mud which accumulates there.

THE TUG *PIONEER* was a familiar sight on Faversham Creek at the end of the nineteenth century and in the early 1900s. This well-worn print has an almost 'Turneresque' appearance in its atmospheric effect, with the paddle-driven tug towing a barge with sails furled. Two further barges, both under sail, can be seen in the distance approaching the wharf at the head of the creek.

FAVERSHAM CEMENT WORKS *c.* 1895, with sailing barges moored in the creek. The factory ceased to operate during the First World War. Further down, past Gillett's tall warehouse, a small sailing ship was probably loading or unloading timber.

A FINE VIEW OF THE CREEK at high tide with the paddle-driven steam tug *Pioneer* at work in 1902. Stacks of imported timber can be seen on the wharfside with Gillett's tall warehouse and the cement works beyond. On the left the cottages of Front Brents still remain in the characterful area that retains its individuality.

THE CREEK with the *Pioneer* alongside the sailing barges moored by the wharf from the cement works to Gillett's warehouse. As ever, children and a dog found the water's edge fascinating in this view which pre-dates the illustration below.

T.U. BARBER'S PHOTOGRAPH OF THE CREEK was used for a postcard date-stamped 1928. The picture was taken after the above illustration as evinced by the trees on the left. The two smaller trees in the previous picture still remain but where the larger tree grew only a stump may be seen in this picture. Also instead of the *Pioneer* working the creek the tug *Noni* is in use. Other aspects of the two views remain quite similar – the warehouses and cement works on the right with sailing barges along the wharf, and the cottages of Front Brents on the left. (see page 34).

GILLETT'S TALL WAREHOUSE, here photographed from the head of the creek, c. 1910, can be seen in the distance with two sailing barges moored alongside the wharf stacked high with timber. Nearer still, above the bridge, there is moored the same vessel seen on page 33 (bottom). To the right of the ship, barrels and wagons are on the wharf by the warehouse, with an overhanging covered gantry which has since been demolished. On the right, out of view, was the barge shed which became converted for use as a roller-skating rink (see page 157, top). There is now a proposal to develop part of this area, including the old gasworks site, in a scheme that would provide about a hundred new homes with consequent tidying and improvement of the tidal basin.

THE FIRST WORLD WAR had led to many innovations and at Faversham the building of concrete ships was undertaken. The narrow width of the creek seen here necessitated broadside launching, which although ungainly was nonetheless impressive. This launch took place on 19 November 1918 shortly after the hostilities of war were ended. It was possibly at the yard of James Pollock & Co. who had commenced shipbuilding on the creek during 1917.

THE VIOLENT SPLASH of the 'sideways-on' launch had a somewhat 'fingers-crossed' look about it. To the left can be seen more lines of bunting, probably on a second vessel at the same stage of completion. In the right-hand distance is the half-filled Faversham gasometer.

THE CONCRETE SHIP AFLOAT. The whole event had been photographed by the redoubtable Mr Hargrave just eight days after the armistice had been signed between Britain and Germany.

LAUNCHING OF THE BARGE *UPLEES* at Uplees in 1898. This vessel was still in use – as a houseboat at Chelsea – in 1963. Sailing barges were built at numerous locations along the Thames and Medway and were often named after some other town or area. Very rarely, as here, the name given was that of the place where the vessel was built.

OARE CREEK about forty years ago with pleasure craft moored at high tide. In the distance the familiar outline of boatyard buildings at Hollow Shore may be seen at the confluence with Faversham Creek. A little to the right of the boatyard stands the Shipwright's Arms (see page 141 bottom).

GEORGE JOHNSON'S BUILDING FIRM AND UNDERTAKERS were situated off St Mary's Road near the railway station. In the picture, probably taken in around 1905, second from left Alfred Beacon, third from left George Carpenter, far right Dan Moore.

WORKSHOP INTERIOR OF GEORGE JOHNSON'S BUILDING FIRM at the turn of the century, showing a variety of hand tools, including jack planes, smoothing planes and plough/rebate planes. The firm closed down in the early 1960s, and the yard, situated behind the old water tower, has been used for a variety of purposes since, including part residential.

COTTON POWDER GIRLS. A group of female munitions workers pictured in their protective clothing. In spite of this protection, the girls often became recognizable by their yellow complexions, causing them sometimes to be referred to as the girls with yellow hands. Their arduous three-mile walk to the works at Uplees was eased in 1916 when the light railway was built from Davington to the factory on the marsh.

OUTSIDE THE OFFICES OF THE COTTON POWDER COMPANY, a meeting of the workers is addressed by a management group on 16 October 1915. Note the long overalls and caps of the female workers, mainly on the right of the group. The office building is believed to have been situated at the Oare works and has now been demolished with practically all other buildings on the site. Many of the men in this photograph were probably killed in April 1916 and the office block was 'burnt out', in the disasterous explosion of that year (see page 117 *et al.*).

THE FACTORY STAFF OF THE COTTON POWDER CO. LTD. gathered outside their office building for a group photograph. When this picture was taken, the company were developing and producing various forms of explosives required in ever-increasing quantities for the war. The explosives industry rapidly declined after the war and the industry that in the early nineteenth century had employed 25 per cent of the male population of Faversham eventually died out in the area.

WHITING BROS. OF OSPRINGE were builders and contractors. They had become a firm of considerable size by 1925 when this photograph was taken of over a hundred employees plus coach drivers taking part in the works outing. The business later became Whiting & Hine and it ceased trading in the 1970s when houses were built on the site. The rails and log on the left of this picture indicate that the background building contained a sawmill where the firm converted timber for its own use. The business also included stonemasonry and undertaking.

SECTION THREE

Country Life and Work

HARVESTING AT PERRY COURT. A once-common scene no longer to be found. Grain crops are now harvested by combine, producing grain on site for tractor-drawn trailers to transport direct to bulk silos. Mechanization has removed the need for a large agricultural labour force, an element of which can be seen here building ricks with sheaves carried on horse-drawn waggons from the fields. Such ricks were later broken down for thrashing to sort the grain from chaff. Perry Court farm is now largely school buildings and playing fields; a further part is under threat of development from yet another trunk road – this one to perhaps run a few yards from, and parallel to, the motorway on the southern boundary.

CAPTIONED 'VIEW IN HOP-LAND NEAR FAVERSHAM', this view, in fact of Selling, glimpses the enviable ruralistic scenes that existed around Faversham in 1911 when overcrowding in community and on roads were unknown. However, there was another side to the picture, unseen here. Low agricultural wages, poor standards of hygiene and the struggle to uplift educational levels were also characteristics of the time.

UPLEES FRUIT FARM, owner Mr E. Knowles, in the early years of this century. The pickers appear to be harvesting the crop from plum trees, and large trees of this type are now far less common in the area than formerly. Modern fruit-growing practice favours smaller trees accessible from the ground or at least from much smaller ladders than those seen here. The many wicker baskets seen in the picture have also been replaced by trays of cardboard or plastic for plums, modern bulk boxes for apples.

BOUGHTON-UNDER-BLEAN, 'High Street'. To the east of Faversham the Roman road, part of the first planned highway in Britain linking London–Canterbury–Richborough, climbs steadily up the incline of Boughton Hill to the still-wooded area of Blean Forest. Seen here at some time in the Edwardian era, this part of the highway can be easily recognised today with the banking and many old houses remaining.

BOUGHTON STREET. Another view looking along the line of Roman road in around 1910. Until this time methods of transport had not changed much in the previous 1900 years, horse-drawn or 'Shanks's pony' being the usual method of locomotion. Certainly on the occasion of this photograph being taken no motor traffic was expected to disturb the peace and serenity of the cows, the donkey with the child rider, lady-cyclist and others.

BOUGHTON STREET. A group of children in front of St Barnabas Church. The village, now much enlarged and extended, has been bypassed by the modern A2 route to Canterbury, affording some relief from the unbearable traffic congestion which filled this scene in later years.

EDWARDIAN LIFE (for some) is exemplified in this photograph of Mountfield at Staple Street, taken by Mr Hargrave around 1904. Unfortunately the cyclist, lady with pram and baby attended by a dog and a man with a horse, cannot be identified. However, the sumptuousness of the Victorian house and the attractiveness of the gardens are witness to a very pleasant lifestyle. The large trees have now gone but the gardens have recently been laid out again.

THE HOLLIES in The Street, Newnham, was built probably in the 1860s by Mr J.G. Coast (see page 50). His daughter, seen here standing at the gate, married Willie John Chapman who sits proudly at the wheel of his new car (one of the first in the district) which was a 12 hp, two-seater 'Star' purchased in 1913 from Standard Quay Garage in Faversham.

W.J. CHAPMAN was a well-known resident of Newnham (see pages 48 & 54). In this photograph, taken in the early years of this century, he is in charge of his own cart providing a conveyance for the local St John's Ambulance Brigade team at a local event, possibly in Faversham. The St John's Ambulance movement was very strong in the area and some villages including Newnham and Doddington fielded enthusiastic units.

MR JOHN GILBERT COAST, who was a builder, was also a Newnham church warden for over thirty years and was a prominent member of the village. With bewhiskered face and Victorian bowler, he is here pictured with a pony outside his house in The Street, Newnham. Mr Coast died on 14 March 1908 (see page 48).

ALTHOUGH FENCED FROM THE IMMEDIATE FRONT LAWN, the trim sheep in this picture demonstrate their secondary use as self-propelled lawnmowers. Despite the eighteenth-century front, the roof and off-centred front door evince the likely existence within of a timber-framed hallhouse with solar cross wing as originally built. This house is known to have been (perhaps still is) in the Faversham area, but it is the only photograph in this book to remain as yet, unidentified.

SHARSTED COURT, properly in the parish of Doddington, but overlooking the village of Newnham. The manor of Sharsted dates from at least the thirteenth century and portions of this very large building are known to date from 1374 or earlier. This view of a portion of the south wing was taken in *c.* 1920 and has much the same appearance today. The de Laune family occupied the house for about 300 years, and latterly it was owned by Canon and Mrs E.H. Wade, whose family remain in occupation.

NASH COURT AT BOUGHTON is a large red-brick mansion *c.* 1700, much restored and embellished in around 1870. At the time of the First World War there was still enough labour available to maintain this jungle-like fernery within a conservatory.

A WELL-PHOTOGRAPHED RABBIT SHOOT took place in the Newnham valley in February 1916. The steeple of Newnham Church can be discerned in the left-hand distance in this view along the Seed road. The event, during wartime, was attended by at least two army personnel and the guns appear to be waiting for rabbits to bolt from the field on the right, although the apparent intent for some shots to be fired over the heads of those lower down the bank would appear to hold some risk for the latter as well.

THE 1916 RABBIT SHOOT IN NEWNHAM. The guns line up waiting for the rabbits to bolt from the bank on the left which was probably being ferreted. The roof line and chimneys of Newnham vicarage can be seen on the skyline above the heads of the army sergeants.

A PAUSE FOR REFRESHMENT at the 1916 rabbit shoot. Mr W.J. Chapman stands centre holding his glass for filling from the stone jar, probably containing cider. On the far right stands Charlie Wilson who had a building and decorating business in Newnham.

THE GAITERED WILLIE JOHN CHAPMAN with his spaniel and double-barrelled twelve-bore, displaying the result of the 1916 Newnham rabbit shoot. The army sergeant on the left leans into the picture wearing an expression which seems to say, 'He didn't shoot them all on his own!' Rabbits caused great damage to crops, but provided a welcome supplement to the meat available for the table, especially during the increasingly bleak years of the First World War (see pages 48 & 49).

BERT FORSTER standing at the door of his garage which he started in The Street, Newnham. The motor-cycle combination is possibly a 'Velocette'. Mr Forster later purchased land opposite and built a new garage where the present Newnham garage operates today. The premises shown here later became a post office which remained until recent years, before reverting to use as a private residence (see page 144 bottom).

NEWNHAM VICARAGE, an early nineteenth-century country vicarage which has happily escaped demolition although it is no longer used by the Church for its original purpose. Now divided into two private homes, it remains an elegant reminder of the days when country clergy were often able to use private funds to erect an imposing gentleman's residence. This inevitably placed them, in the eyes of the working population at least, in a similar category to the squire.

STORIES VARY ABOUT HOW MANY BAKERS USED TO EXIST IN NEWNHAM. It was a time of course when villages were far more independent and self-sufficient than they can be today. Here is Bill Anderson, baker of Newnham, at the front door of his house in Newnham Street in 1908 with his front room serving nicely for his retail trade. The house, now reverted to fully residential accommodation, can be easily recognised today.

CALICO HOUSE is well-known for the exterior wall decoration dated 1712 but this does not refer to the structure as seen from the road. The front aspect probably represents the remodelling carried out by Stephen Hulkes about 100 years earlier. However, parts of the building are much older, perhaps dating back to the thirteenth century. Despite this, these children at the beginning of this century, peeping out from the seventeenth-century porch and lining up across the road, were more interested in the photographer's contortions beneath his black cloth. Large straw hats were obviously *de rigueur* among the girls who greatly outnumbered the boys.

THE STREET, EASTLING, a splendid photograph featuring the post office in the care of T.J. Doughty who later purchased the empty butcher's shop in Doddington for his son S.W. Doughty. The widely renowned butcher's shop at Doddington continues in business under the care of Douglas, T.J.'s grandson, thus continuing a local association of many years standing. This group outside the Eastling shop in around 1911 displays a delightful glimpse of rural life including three forms of human-assisted transport. There is what appears to be a folding pushchair, a hugh wheeled and self-propelled conveyance occupied by a be-whiskered gentleman, and a large-wheeled pram by the door of the shop. Another feature often found in old photographs of village streets is the lazy dog lying in the dusty road.

EASTLING was the birthplace of Edward Hasted, born in 1732, who became a famous historian of Kent. Eastling Manor, (see below) shown here in around 1920, was probably nearly 400 years old when Hasted was born nearby, for this house of seventeenth-century appearance fronts an aisled hall with cross-wing. This places it into the fourteenth century and is therefore contemporary in period with another ancient building nearby (see page 61).

THIS POSTCARD of around 1900, simply titled 'Old House, Eastling' provides an example of the value of studying old illustrations of buildings when evaluating their architectural development. Fenced around with sheep hurdles it may have been divided into farm cottages at the time. Taking away the additions of chimneys and the seventeenth-century far wing with half-hipped roof, there would be left the central one-storey hall with two-storey solar cross-wing being part, or even all, of an original hallhouse already over 500 years old when this picture was taken. The building is in fact Eastling Manor (see above).

ST MARY'S CHURCH AT EASTLING in around 1910. There are late Norman and thirteenth-century features in this prettily situated church which was unfortunately over-restored in the mid-nineteenth century, possibly following a fire. However, the attractive rural surroundings alone ensure the delight of a visit in Spring or on any fine day.

EASTLING RECTORY, pictured around 1915. On the far left two maids stand watching the photographer record this scene of an English country parsonage among the roses. It is typical of many such country cleric's homes built in the early Victorian period, only to be found over-large and too expensive to maintain by the Church in this century. It is now in private residential use.

DIVAN COURT AT EASTLING around 1913 with a tennis court marked out on the lawn. The smiling gentleman was almost certainly Mr Harry F. Boucher, seen here holding back a huge dog of Great Dane proportions whose interest in the photographer may well have excused the latter some nervousness. The creeper-covered house with sash windows encompasses, as so often, an earlier structure belied by the outside appearance. The architectural evidence confirms that the house was built as a hall-house with solar cross-wing, and a brief examination has revealed that later enlargement has taken place with a complete replacement of the front. However, enough survives, particularly in the roof where there are two fine moulded crownposts over the solar, to confirm the origins of the house. Excitingly, recent restoration work by the present owners has revealed a Tudor stone fireplace, inserted into what appears to be an earlier fireplace opening (possibly for a brazier) in the solar which is part of the original house. The wooden 'jambs' of the earlier fireplace have carved finials in 'Decorated' style, indicating that the house originates from the fourteenth century. Impressive corroboration is provided in historical record. Divan Court was earlier called Diven Court, itself corrupted from Dive Court. John Dive held the estate in the reign of Henry III (1216–1272). The heirs of John Dive continued ownership in the same name until around 1380. Divan (Diven) survives in the name of the building and strongly supports a postulated date of no later than 1380 for the original structure, which could possibly be more precisely dated by detailed survey.

AN OVERALL VIEW OF NEWNHAM from a favoured viewpoint on the hill leading to Sharsted. On the left there are sheaves standing in the field by the hill leading to Eastling. A horse and cart stands sleepily in the street and the council houses at Wineycock beyond the church are not yet built. Yet much remains the same: the church and The George still face each other, the one having spiritual refreshment on offer to all, the other providing refreshment of a more secular kind.

NEWNHAM CHURCH around 1905. Its shingled spire (of uncharacteristic appearance for Kent) peeps invitingly over the folds of the valley slopes on the approach from Faversham. There is a warmth of welcome at this church, one feels it must always have been so but apparently not, for in the seventeenth century the fabric was almost ruinous and open to weather and birds. Architecturally, much of the interior shows the narrow perception of the Victorian (1868) restoration, but even this is absorbed in an atmosphere that quietly withstands human follies with forgiveness.

AT NEWNHAM in 1921, E. Hills the postmaster proudly stood outside his 'Supply Stores' and post office with other members of his family. There was a motor-cycle and wicker sidecar with two occupants, and an altogether safer-looking pony and trap held by his daughter. In addition to drapery and clothing, Mr Hills maintained the usual wide selection of goods then available in village stores. Next door was, and still is, The George village pub. Further down the road, on the right-hand side, can be seen the various buildings of the forge and wheelwright's. The post office has been situated in other premises in Newnham over the years, both before and after this photograph was taken. In more recent times it returned once more to Mr Hills' former shop, only for it to be closed down, leaving Newnham with no post office at all.

NEWNHAM in around 1910 with many features distinguishable today. The timber and brick house on the right remains, as does The George further on. The church is featured on page 63 and to the left, between Seed Road and Eastling Lane, can be seen the decorative bargeboards of the Victorian Cottage which served as the policeman's house for a time. Between the photographer and the horse and cart, on the left, the ground now has new houses upon it, but then the bewhiskered and amply built farrier, with trousers trussed below the knees, grinned amiably upon photographers and the world in general. The dogs in the dusty road had yet to hear about traffic.

ALFRED HUMPHREY, who came from Wrotham, photographed in his wheelwright's yard at Newnham in the early days of the First World War. Alfred is the left-hand of the three taller figures, the other two being employees of the business. Alfred's three sons are (left to right) Fred the youngest, Alfred the eldest and John. The three boys grew up to continue the business, which included local building work and undertaking. For the latter, coffins were made on the premises and pall-bearers provided. There was a forge and well-equipped workshop, timber was felled locally and converted in the yard sawmill. Fred became a notable craftsman in joinery and carving; surviving examples of his work are highly regarded today. Unfortunately the younger Alfred died following a working accident, but the business continued to provide a valuable service in the rural area until about 1970. The fifteenth-century yeoman's house survives just behind where the photographer stood to take this picture. New houses now stand where craftsmen once toiled (see facing page).

IN NEWNHAM at the end of the First World War this picture was taken of a mother sitting on a rustic garden seat in her garden. Kate Victoria Jarvis of Downe Court in Doddington had married Alfred Humphrey (see facing page) and is here seen with her youngest son Fred and baby Kate upon her knee.

BARRACK ROW, in Newnham, and shown here before the First World War, was built in the mid-1840s from materials salvaged from barracks demolished at Sheerness. The row of cottages mark the site of a fire which occurred in 1844, destroying 14 houses, and leaving 70 people homeless. The disaster was recorded by the vicar James Bower who noted in the church register that although three fire engines from Sittingbourne and Faversham quenched the flames, it was impossible to prevent the loss of property and goods although no lives were lost.

AT BADLESMERE, a sale of work which took place on 19 August 1913 holds great interest to us now in a detailed study of the dress, hairstyles and the industry of the seated group.

QUEEN COURT FARM in Ospringe was acquired by Shepherd Neame & Co. in 1944 in order to grow their own hops. The Manor of Queen Court is a very ancient one known to be part of the possessions of Odo, the half-brother of William of Normandy in 1080. The timbered portion of building seen in this picture of 1948 is the left-hand part of Queen Court which is a 'Wealden' style hall-house, judged by outside appearance to be about 1400 or even a little earlier in date. The middle distance, beyond the stockyard, shows the position of the oast-house since demolished.

THE OAST-HOUSE with three oast kilns, formerly on the north side of Vicarage Lane, Ospringe. No trace remains of this structure, but its precise site behind Queen Court can be determined by reference to the house, and the extant agricultural building with pulley hoist that still overhangs the verge of the lane.

A WIDE ASSORTMENT OF HATS, picnic baskets, cooking utensils and babies are evident in this picture of ladies engaged in training hop bines on the poles near Faversham in about 1910/11. The pots, pans, baskets etc. confirm that mothers were prepared to spend their day's work in the fields, feeding themselves and their children there also. Mrs Hilda Tyler (née Burden) is standing, fourth from the left. Next to her, third from the left, is Mrs Anne Tyler (née Cox). The photograph was taken by Theo Barber of Preston Street.

RABBITS were a serious menace to farmers (as they are again now in some areas following their re-emergence from the years of myxomatosis to which they are developing a resistant strain). Shoots were organised to reduce the rabbit population, the guns at Mr Clark's shoot were pictured on 3 January 1910 waiting for the rabbits to bolt from their ferreted burrows.

ALTHOUGH TITLED 'THE BROOKS', no stream now exists in the Ospringe valley. The line of pollarded willows through the centre of this picture in 1905 marked the course of the brook, some of the old houses remain and, with Ospringe Church in the distance, they combined in this view to form an attractive countryside scene framed by trees. Now a motorway cuts the valley in the far distance, the willows have gone, and the immediate foreground of path and Mutton Lane is forever filthy and littered with household waste. A visit there is a depressing event.

IN OSPRINGE a group of village boys watched the photographer with interest in 1905, when this view was taken across the stream, with the windmill adjacent to the millhouse on the west side of Water Lane. The windmill was built at the end of the eighteenth century on a very high brick base that itself was three storeys tall, reaching above the height of the nearby houses. The timber 'smock' type windmill was erected on this base, the height thus gained probably being necessary for the sails to catch the wind in the valley bottom situation. The mill was demolished in 1915. The photograph reveals how the stream was embanked to keep the level of water high before entry into the millpond. Mutton Lane on the right crossed the stream by a ford, and out of sight to the right the millpond was used to provide power for a watermill on the east side of Water Lane.

SECTION FOUR

Transport

THE RAILWAY STATION as built in the mid-nineteenth century was a substantial building, as seen here before 1896 when rebuilding commenced. This photograph epitomizes the leisured pace of life beyond the railway. Speedy carriage of people and goods was the prerogative of the railway companies; outside the station entrance the old ways still persisted. After an exhilarating, but sometimes alarmingly fast, journey by train, perhaps many passengers sank thankfully into the more familiar seats aboard the sedately horse-drawn conveyances on the station forecourt (see below and pages 17, 75 & 76).

FAVERSHAM STATION in 1880. The Preston Street level crossing was still in use and the station buildings seen on the right were the rear (south side) of those pictured above, which incorporated the station-master's home. There is a distinctly 'country' appearance about the platforms, and beyond can be seen the currently named Delbridge House which had been in use as a private school for over thirty years, until almost the time of this photograph (see pages 17, 75 & 76).

ON FAVERSHAM RAIL SIDINGS, a South-East and Chatham Railway steam locomotive is depicted in this faded and indistinct photograph which is undated. The locomotive appears to be a 'Europa' class 2–4–0, designed by Kirtley in the late nineteenth century. The picture cannot be earlier than 1900 following the formation of the SE & CR.

FAVERSHAM RAIL SIDINGS in the 1920s. A locomotive has collided with a signals' gantry and work is under way to prevent the structure toppling over. The extent of the Faversham sidings can be judged from this view which includes the four 'through' roads provided after the 1896 station reconstruction (see above and pages 17, 74 & 76).

THE CONSTRUCTION OF FORBES ROAD AND THE RAILWAY BRIDGE in 1897/8 (see pages 17, 74 & 75) necessitated the removal of a considerable depth of earth. Just how much may be judged from this contemporary picture taken on the south side of the bridge. The 'pick, shovel and heave-it' method, with horse and cart for transportation, also reminds us how the bulk of the vast engineering and construction works of the nineteenth century were tackled, before the advent of the recent, and comparatively short, mechanical digger and bulldozer era.

Bottom right.
GEORGE BEER AND RIGDEN'S BREWERY delivered 'Kent's Best' in a steam lorry known as a 'Clayton Undertype' in 1923. Pictured here at the Court Street brewery premises are Jack Kirby the transport foreman and Bob Quantrell the driver with his mate Fred Sparrow. The front of the solid-tyred vehicle featured three attractive oil lamps that would have served to give warning of the vehicle's approach in the unlikely event of it not being heard.

THIS DELIVERY VEHICLE OF RIGDEN'S BREWERY in 1904 was virtually a steam traction engine with a design modification, involving smaller drive wheels to facilitate the addition of a load-bearing platform on the back. The result was a very workmanlike job with even a faintly 'racy' looking appearance – belied by the inscription on the side of the engine stating that speed was limited to 5 mph. The identity of the operators is unknown, the makers of the vehicle appear to have been Foden.

A VIEW OF OARE with Rigden's The Castle pub on the right. In the foreground may be seen the level crossing gates formerly serving the light railway line from Davington which was used to convey workers to the gunpowder works at Uplees marsh, (see pages 40 & 41). This photograph was taken by Theo Barber in around 1920.

THE ROAD FROM OARE TO HARTY FERRY in the 1920s was frequented by people using the ferry which closed in the 1950s. Any intending passengers on the south side of the Swale had to stand between two posts on the sea wall and wave across the water towards Harty Ferry Inn on Sheppey. Only then would the ferryman set out to collect his fares and row them across, although his task was later eased by the addition of an outboard motor on his craft. Others used the road also; fishermen, workers at the fulminate of mercury factory of which there is now no trace, anyone needing access to the coastguard cottages or even perhaps the TA gun practice platform. Nature reserves and an ever-increasing number of boating enthusiasts ensure a renewed and continued busy use of this road, which had become, until a few years ago, a little-used byway.

PICTURED IN NEWTON ROAD, this steam engine had a load-carrying capacity which could also evidently be tipped by means of a winding gear controlled by the driver. The side of the tipping body bore the legend: 'Associated Portland Cement Co. Faversham 1910'. The cement works ceased operating at the creekside works in the First World War.

THIS LORRY TRANSPORTED EXPLOSIVES from the powder works at Uplees to Dover docks during the First World War. The driver, seen here at the front of his vehicle in 1918, was Bert Gurr who had been invalided out of the army after being gassed. Bert was also a member of the Home Guard unit (shown on page 128) and was therefore one of many men who had found themselves donning uniform to serve in two harrowing world wars.

PERCY BEALE NEAME purchased one of the earliest traction engines made by Aveling and Porter of Rochester in 1874. This was used to deliver Shepherd Neame's beer on the longer journeys, the furthest at that time being the 13 miles to Ashford. The traction engine with trailer in tow was preceded by a man on foot equipped with red flag to give warning of the engine's approach. The engine under steam is seen here with the driver F. Burney.

THE USE OF HORSE-DRAWN DRAYS and mechanically-powered transport for deliveries had a considerable overlap at Shepherd Neame. From 1874 until 1968 both methods were in use. In 1926 a Fordson tractor and trailer with drivers Stan Brenchley and George Tillman was used for local deliveries. It was described as slow but reliable!

STEAM POWER is seen here in 1927 in this picture of a solid-tyred steam 'Sentinel' which remained in use for Shepherd Neame brewery deliveries until the late 1930s.

AN EARLY SHEPHERD NEAME DELIVERY LORRY in service 1930–35 was this 'Thorneycroft' with part wooden body. The crew of that time were Ernie Culver and George Stokes.

A VERY WORKMANLIKE APPEARANCE is exhibited by this Shepherd and Neame 'Thorneycroft' delivery vehicle used in 1946–50. Finely panelled wooden doors to the cab with lined engine cowling and other front details make an old-fashioned contrast to the more modern looking load carrying body. No need for the company name, – 'Malt and Hops Only' told all.

AT THE SHEPHERD NEAME FAVERSHAM BREWERY this Thorneycroft 'Bulldog' delivery lorry was in use until the late 1960s.

MANY OF THE SHEPHERD NEAME DRAY HORSES were bred on the farm of Mr Percy Beale Neame at Dunkirk in the late nineteenth century. This scene in 1948 outside the Faversham brewery stables (formerly on the site of the present bottling hall) shows horses; Punch, Tommy and Duke with their handlers Sid Chittenden, George Sweeting and Wally Bosley.

SHEPHERD NEAME continued to use horses for deliveries for many years as well as using motor transport. The horse era ended at the brewery in 1968 and Charlie, the last of the dray horses, appears in this picture taken a few years earlier in 1963, outside The Castle Inn in West Street at Faversham. The cart was loaded with wooden bottle crates and oak casks, how quickly another era has passed!

SECTION FIVE

Events, Celebrations and War

ST JOHN'S AMBULANCE BRIGADE CHURCH PARADE, 1 July 1906. Pictured at the north end of Preston Street, Dr Evers (wearing a grey bowler) can be seen at the forefront of the parade passing the front of the Dolphin Hotel. The building, together with others of earlier date, has sadly been replaced by badly designed modern retail premises.

THE WINTER OF 1894/5 produced these conditions in Faversham Creek, where the ice was both very thick and uncommon enough to excite the curiosity of the locals pictured here. Changing climatic conditions in recent years have made this degree of sustained frost very unusual. However such are the vagaries of East Kent weather, with its exposed situation to north-east blizzards, that one never knows. . . .

THE GUILDHALL resplendently arrayed in celebration of Queen Victoria's Diamond Jubilee in 1897. The handsome gas lamp standard is well seen in this picture, but the only sign of life – the rather forlorn-looking horse in harness – appears unimpressed with the appearance of grandeur around it (see pages 11 & 12). The reign of 60 years accomplished in 1897 by Queen Victoria, and celebrated throughout the British Empire, coincided with the period at which that empire extended all over the world, and on which quite literally 'the sun never set'.

FLOODING caused by abnormally high tides remains a hazard near the creek even today. In November 1897 the effect was both extensive and severe: the horse by the tree in the middle foreground appears to be standing in about two feet of water. To the right of the church spire can be seen the two chimneys of Rigden's Brewery (now Whitbread's), with the tall brewery building on the right. The large house with columns and cornice framing the door is Bridge House, once The Brents Coffee Tavern. There also remains the bracket lamp above the door: in this picture it looks upon the flood water in a normally tranquil scene; now it surveys a changed world with busy motor traffic crossing the bridge over the creek (beyond the horse in this picture).

THE SAME FLOOD as in the previous illustration, this time featuring buildings that used to exist near the creekside in the Conduit Street area close to Shepherd Neame's Brewery, which almost certainly was the source of the empty barrels floating down the street. The large advertising board directs the onlooker to go to J. Miskin's household stores in Court Street.

CURLING'S ALLEY FIRE, 28 May 1908. The resourceful W. Hargrave, photographer of Faversham, was able to persuade members of the fire brigade, police force and others to stand amid the still smoking ruins of a large fire which destroyed much property behind the cottage hospital and former chapel.

CURLING'S ALLEY. This overall view of the aftermath of the fire (see above) illustrates how much more extensive this conflagration could have been amid the congested, haphazard and largely wooden buildings on this site. Prompt fire-fighting must have averted an even worse disaster.

'A' TROOP OF THE ROYAL EAST KENT MOUNTED RIFLES at the ball in the lecture hall of Faversham Institute on 26 February 1906. The hall had a sprung floor for dancing, making it ideal for occasions such as this. W. Hargrave, photographer, and to whom we are indebted for so many photographs of old Faversham, noted on the edge of this picture 'Flashlight Photo' and his name, etc. Presumably flash powder was used, and a fairly big charge at that, for this interior. We see here a sea of faces, still, serious and intent, waiting for the flash. How they must have erupted into relieved laughter after the flare and puff of smoke! Alas, we have no picture of that moment.

GENERAL ELECTION, December 1910. The crowd gathered on 10 December outside the Guildhall after the election won by Mr Granville Wheler, the Conservative candidate. The first-floor windows of Sidney Peters' premises provided grandstand viewing of the numbers below (described in the newspaper report as several thousand) awaiting the outcome of the contest. The result was read out (between the cheers and shouts of the crowd) by Mr Guy Tassell. Mr Wheler polled 6,897 votes, a majority of 1,786 over his opponent, Liberal candidate Mr George Nicholls who described himself as 'the working man's candidate'.

Bottom left.
THE FAVERSHAM ADULT SCHOOL was founded in 1903 with strong local support. After five successful years the anniversary was celebrated in 1908 with this procession seen passing along East Street between Cooksditch and the Queen's Parade shops which were built in 1901. Half-hidden by the banner is a Victorian house at the foot of St Mary's Road. Beyond that is the former Faversham College which still bears its faded title across the façade. It was at that time a girls' school under the administration of the Misses Lush.

GENERAL ELECTION DAY, December 1910. Voting took place on the ninth and on the following day, Saturday the tenth, which was chilly and wet, a crowd gathered outside the Guildhall where motor cars and carriages awaited. The window of Webb's the jeweller was well stocked but held no interest for anyone on this occasion. On the far right, in Middle Row, the hanging sign of The Star Inn can just be discerned. Mr Granville Wheler, the Conservative candidate, held the seat with a reduced majority over the Liberal candidate Mr George Nicholls.

GENERAL ELECTION 1910. A fine turnout of traction engines and wagons bedecked with flags and bunting in support of the successful candidate, Mr Granville Wheler. Regrettably, it is impossible to discern any names on the vehicles and trucks, but probably they were owned by the Shepherd Neame brewery who used them for deliveries when they were not being pressed into service for elections and carrying their employees to the poll!

IN THE 1910 GENERAL ELECTION Mr Granville Wheler was the successful conservative candidate. The result had been announced on 10 December and on that evening a carriage with Mr Wheler had been hauled by his supporters in a torchlight procession from Ospringe to Market Place. In celebration of his success Mr Wheler had printed this postcard of himself and his wife on their estate, in order to send thanks to his many helpers.

PRESTON STREET, 30 July 1905. The Church Lads Brigade passing number 79, occupied by E. Knowles, whose twin-gabled and jettied sixteenth-century shop had no space wasted in the pursuit of self-advertisement – 'Fruit Grower, Fruit Importer, also at Dover and Whitstable', and so on. Three attractively bracketed lamps hung from the façade to illuminate the produce display on open days and other scroll work can be seen on the street lamp-standards. Number 79 survived until the mid-sixties when it was demolished, but this good view of the street's east frontage enables many other buildings to be identified with existing structures (page 98).

THE ANGLE OF THIS PHOTOGRAPH conveys a first impression that the float was moving downhill. It was in fact being pulled uphill in Newton Road where the background houses may still be identified. Second prize was awarded to this float, drawn by a two-horse team in the celebrations following Coronation Day on 22 June 1911. A suitably-attired 'John Bull' is seated at the front of the float which was called 'The British Isles' (see pages 99, 100 & 101).

THE TERRITORIAL ARMY proved to be of great importance in the First World War, as it did again some 25 years later. In the year preceding the outbreak of the earlier conflict the Territorials held a church parade at the parish church, and are here seen passing the police station in Church Road with the former garden of Rigden's Brewery over the wall on the left. The parade was led by Stanley C. Berry on 6 April 1913 (see page 106).

IN SCHOOL ROAD the Faversham Scouts mourned the death of Scoutmaster Grainge from Number 6, as they hauled the coffin in the funeral procession on 28 September 1911. Scoutmaster Grainge, aged 24 years, had died in St Catherine's Hospital at Ramsgate. He had worked for nine years at Mills Bros. the clothiers in Court Street. The No. 1 Troop of The Faversham Company of Boy Scouts hauled the coffin of their scoutmaster on a wheeled bier. Numbers 2 and 3 Troops also attended. The photograph was taken by W. Hargrave who was also a scoutmaster.

AFTER A CHURCH PARADE on 23 May 1909, members of the congregation were pictured making their way home along Court Street, past the premises of Child & Son and the offices of Shepherd Neame (see page 140 top). A study of fashion in the dress worn by the throng reveals a range from Victorian survival to the dashing Edwardian rig of the day. The array of ladies' hats was charming and everyone sported headgear of some sort.

ANOTHER OPPORTUNISTIC PHOTOGRAPH BY W. HARGRAVE shows the volunteers, led by their splendid band, marching away from their church parade on 30 July 1905 – the same occasion as that illustrated on page 94. Here the volunteers are at the lower (northern) end of Preston Street, passing the Dolphin Hotel and watched by at least a trio of gaily-dressed and admiring young ladies.

KING GEORGE V was crowned on the 22 June 1911. A procession with many floats was organised in Faversham on the following day. This picture shows the horse-drawn display representing 'The British Isles' waiting at the top of St John's Road. The wall at the top end of the road borders the railway. On the right can be seen a gable bearing the legend 'General Repairs' on some upper doors. The building is still in use today for the same trade of small building and repair work. Changing fashions may be glimpsed in the dress of the two ladies in the road beyond the float. The left-hand figure wears Edwardian dress of wide hat, three-quarter length coat and long skirt. The right-hand lady is attired in Victorian style with bonnet and voluminous full coat or skirt. (See pages 95 top, 100 & 101.)

CORONATION DAY. King George V was crowned on 22 June 1911. There was great celebrating in the town on that and the following days (see pages 95 top, 99 & 101). On the recreation ground the crowd (in a magnificent display of hats) was being led in community singing in front of the bandstand. The gentleman conducting the proceedings was gamely perched upon a makeshift rostrum of what appears to be a box on the top of a kitchen table. This rickety construction was grimly held in position by a hefty-looking assistant. And the band played on. . . .

HAPPILY MANY PHOTOGRAPHS SURVIVE of the extensive King George V Coronation celebrations that took place in Faversham. In this photograph, taken on the Recreation Ground, various floats and displays have been judged. From the local fire brigade float to small girls wheeling decorated prams and pushchairs, everything and everyone was gaily attired, and there were crowns and pictures of the new King and Queen. Young Ivy Butler (who was to become Mrs Tong) stands on the left holding a decorated streamer attached to the float awarded second prize in Class 4. With Ivy, was very probably her sister Winifred (later Mrs Wyles). (See pages 95 top, 99 & 100.)

EARLIER IN THIS CENTURY, Empire Day used to be celebrated throughout the British Empire each year on the 24 May, the anniversary of Queen Victoria's birthday. The festival was first introduced in order to encourage the training of schoolchildren to become good citizens. In 1923 a school group were pictured in the national dress of 'Ireland'.

ON THE EMERGENCY TRAINING EXERCISE held by the VAD (TF) 4th County Kent at Easter in 1913, the 'wounded' were photographed making their way towards the nearest 'field hospital', possibly at Barrow Green. The volunteer scouts/casualties, appropriately wearing heavy bandages, appear to be far outnumbered by their rescuers (See following pages).

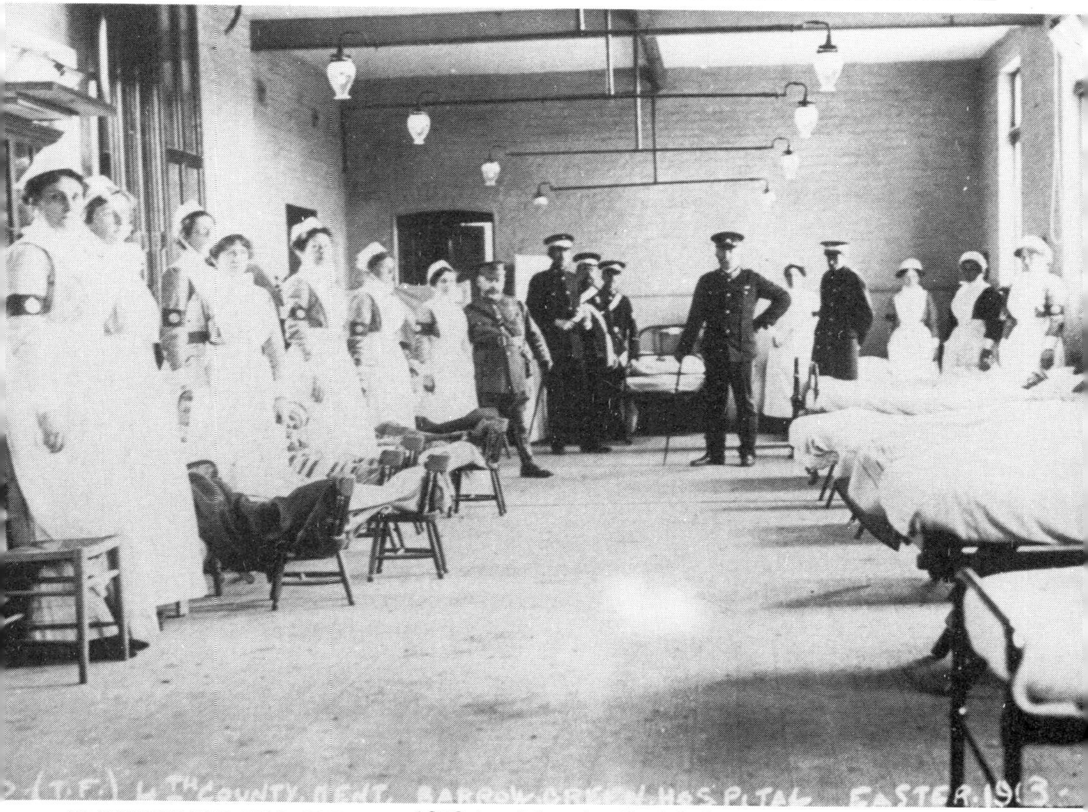

AN EXERCISE WAS HELD AT EASTER 1913 involving the St John's Ambulance brigade and nursing units, members of which are seen here in one of the temporary 'hospitals' staffed by the VAD (TF) 4th County of Kent. This 'hospital' was situated at Barrow Green, on the outer edge of the area covered by this book, between Greenstreet and Teynham, the whole of which is now generally referred to as Teynham. Although there was a wooden hut at Barrow Green used by the St John's Ambulance Brigade, the building used for this exercise was almost certainly the nearby school (cf. page 105) and the photograph shows the folding partition used to divide the large room into two classrooms during normal term time. The nurses are shown wearing their Voluntary Aid Detachment armbands. A Territorial Force (now TA) officer is present as are members of the St John's Ambulance Brigade, the senior member of which was probably Mr Ray. Bed 'patients' for practising upon were obtained by pressing children into service, two of whom could not resist peeping at the photographer from behind the skirts of the nurses on the left. The premises have now been converted into a club with restaurant and leisure facilities.

AMBULANCE BRIGADES were well supported in the town and surrounding villages. In 1914 a Field Day was held involving organisations over a wide area in order to rehearse emergency procedures which included the utilisation of trains and other transport. The need for such exercises seemed increasingly important as the threat of war loomed closer and indeed, although these volunteers could not have foreseen it so soon, the outbreak of the First World War was only about four months distant.

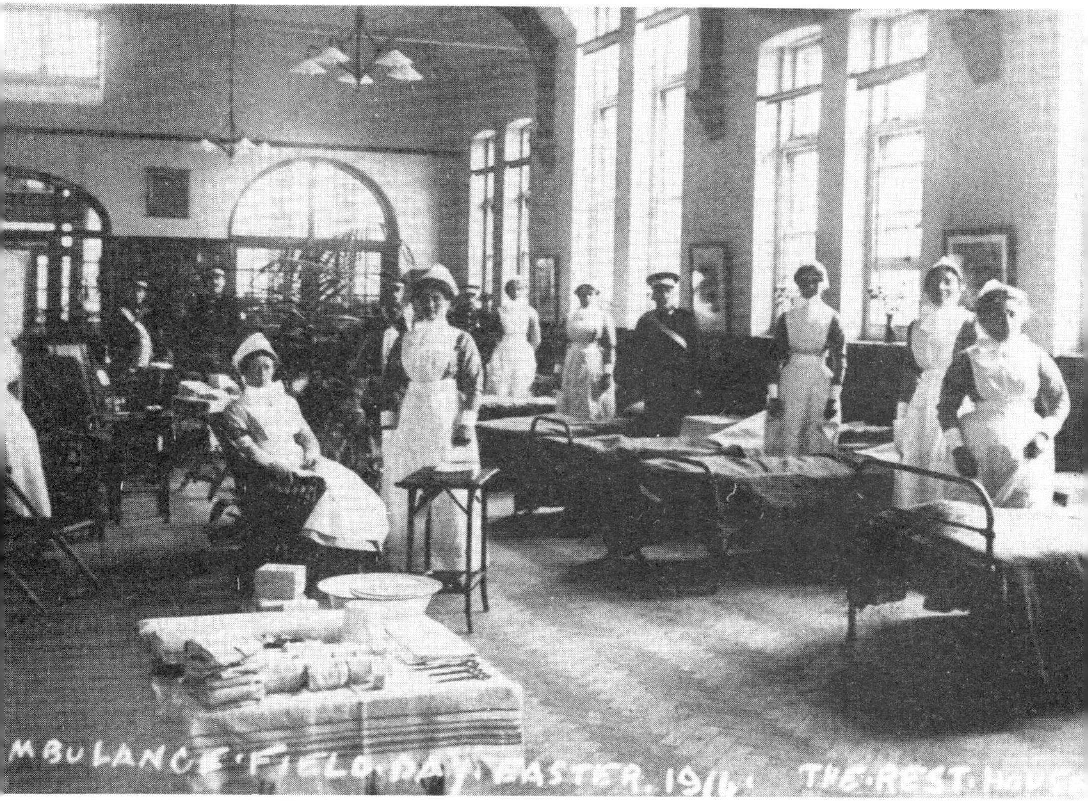

AMBULANCE FIELD DAY, Easter 1914. 'The Rest House', which was in fact the hall of the present County Primary Infants School in Ethelbert Road, put to use during the school Easter holiday. The hall remains architecturally very much the same with the addition of modern lighting. In this scene the nursing staff await the arrival of 'casualties' who were usually scouts and others 'volunteered' for the task (cf. page 103).

BOY SCOUTS are entering the parish church of St Mary of Charity along the pathway lined by soldiers and the waiting congregation on 6 April 1913. The church is famed for the steeple built in 1799 by Charles Beazley and is a more pleasing example of the type at St-Dunstan-in-the-East built by Christopher Wren. However, it is an expensive crowning glory to maintain. Rotting ironwork dating from a Victorian restoration has necessitated recent remedial work on the steeple at great cost (see page 95 bottom).

LEES COURT at Sheldwich was built in the mid-seventeenth century at the behest of Sir George Sondes. The architect is generally acknowledged to have been Inigo Jones who incorporated an earlier house within the overall design. This view was taken in *c.* 1907.

ON THE NIGHT OF 20 November 1910 a disasterous fire burnt Lees Court to a shell despite the efforts of the fire brigades and the effects of a snowstorm. Seen here on the following morning, smoke still rises from the devastated building.

LEES COURT FIRE 20 November 1910. Subsequent to the fire further demolition work had to be undertaken to render the structure safe. The comprehensiveness of the destruction can be judged from this photograph which shows that a large section of the front was lost including the central doorway. However, the house was rebuilt in exactly matching style within a few years, the only outward difference in appearance being the chimneys.

FOLLOWING THE LEES COURT FIRE OF 1910, rebuilding resulted in the completion of an elegant structure once more. The house today is divided into residential units in private ownership. This side view of the house, long after the restoration following the fire, shows the difference between the new chimneys and the originals as seen on page 107 (top).

LEES COURT. As with many other large houses in the area accommodation was given over for the convalescence of casualties returned from the front in the First World War (see p. 110). This group of 'walking wounded' from various units, together with some members of the nursing staff, were arranged on the front terrace steps of the rebuilt Lees Court for the convenience of Mr Hargrave's camera on 30 May 1915. An interesting detail is the difference to be discovered in the front door, which has a fixed window light above, compared with the pre-1910 fire front door of full height (page 107 top).

THE MOUNT, in use as a hospital for the First World War wounded, listed VAD (Voluntary Aid Detachment) No. 140. The house had been the residence of Percy Beale Neame, who was a partner, and later the principal, of Shepherd Neame's brewery from 1869 to 1913. The present cricket ground and open space was formerly much bigger, extending to Upper St Ann's Road and including the horse-chestnut trees bordering that road.

STAFF AND WOUNDED SOLDIERS of the First World War pictured outside The Mount on 31 March 1915. The eastern part of The Mount grounds was developed as a small estate of private houses between the wars. The cricket ground had long been maintained by Percy Neame for the use of Faversham Cricket Club and facilities for the sport, together with football pitches, were provided again when the field and house were acquired by the Borough Council in 1936. It is now known as King George's Playing Field.

THE FIRST WORLD WAR began for Britain on 4 August 1914 with the declaration of war on Germany. On the following day in Faversham some of the atmosphere of that time was captured in this scene in Preston Street, where guns and supplies were being moved towards the railway station. The scene is confused, chaotic even; the worried and serious expressions of onlookers contain a hint of some impossible knowledge of the awful slaughter that was to come. Faversham scenes of processions in carnival-like spirit are more usually to be found, but this picture shows the town in more sombre mood.

THE 3RD WEST LANCS BRIGADE, ROYAL FIELD ARTILLERY, was in Kent for a time during the First World War. Lt. Harold Gilroy Beazley of the 12th Battery married Miss Edith Birkmyre Langlands. The ceremony took place on 16 January 1915 at SS Peter and Paul, Ospringe. Lt. Beazley, who was the second officer of the unit to be married at Ospringe Church, and Miss Langlands both came from Cheshire, but presumably a wedding nearer home was not possible in the war conditions of the time. A large assembly of guests and onlookers gathered. Cars were provided for the principal guests, but an open coach, pulled by six horses with postillions from the regiment, was to convey the bride and groom from the church.

OSPRINGE CHURCH, 16 January 1915, the Beazley/Langlands wedding. The officer guests gathered outside the lych-gate before the wedding, with (possibly) the bareheaded groom standing centre.

OSPRINGE CHURCH, 16 January 1915, the Beazley/Langlands wedding. The bride and groom leave the church under a guard of honour provided by Lt. Beazley's comrades.

OSPRINGE, 16 January 1915. After the wedding Lt. and Mrs Beazley are seen in their open coach drawn by six horses being driven at a cracking pace down Water Lane. The spray is flying and onlookers press back against the fence on the right. On the left caps are waved and salutes given outside the Ospringe Cadet Rifle Range, built in 1910 (being auctioned for 'development' at the time of writing). A little further on can be seen the entry of the stream to the roadway, where it passed under a footbridge after leaving the millpond out of sight and contained at a higher level, to the left.

THE FOOTBRIDGE, glimpsed in the illustration on page 114, can be seen here on the east side of Water Lane where the stream emerged from the millpond. The timber-framed sixteenth-century cottages on the left still exist, as does the Victorian terrace further down on the same side. Prone to occasionally drying up, the stream was diverted through a culvert in 1962, since which time the drop in the water-table has led to its disappearance in the valley to the south of Ospringe. Modern bungalows now stand where the millpond was situated.

THE MALL IN WARTIME. In November 1915 two houses, numbers 56 and 58, were occupied by soldiers, some of whom can be seen outside with their field artillery pieces and ammunition wagons. During the war, troops were billeted in many houses with some larger ones utilized for hospitals accommodating war wounded (see pages 109 & 110).

LORD HARRIS of Belmont and cricketing fame, attended the sports meeting held at Faversham by the 3rd West Lancs. RFA at Easter 1915. The 3rd West Lancs. artillery brigade was a Territorial Force called to service in the war. They trained in the area and were prominent in local life for a time in the early years of the war (see pages 112, 113, 114 & 120). Lord Harris lived at Belmont near Faversham and held various important government positions in the late nineteenth century, eventually becoming Lord-in-Waiting to Queen Victoria from 1895 to 1900. He further endeared himself to Kent by fostering the cricketing fortunes of the county, and indeed was player-captain for a number of years. He also played for England against Australia on four occasions. In 1895 he was elected president of the Marylebone Cricket Club.

THE FAVERSHAM 1916 EXPLOSION. During the First World War the production of munitions was of vital national importance and the Faversham works endeavoured to meet the increasing demands made upon it. Tragedy fell upon the local community on Sunday 2 April 1916 when a colossal explosion at the marshside explosives works at Uplees killed 108 male workers. Female employees did not work on Sundays, but the deaths and injuries devastated many local families. On the Thursday following the accident a funeral procession formed up by the Guildhall. This picture shows fire brigade members waiting to take their place.

THE FAVERSHAM 1916 EXPLOSION. The procession under way led by funeral music and flowers. There were many silent and grieving onlookers, among whom were service personnel as well as civilians. Shops were closed and shuttered, a Union Jack flew at half-mast. The pressures of war were taking their toll at home as well as at the front in France.

THE FAVERSHAM 1916 EXPLOSION. Soldiers and mourners filing past the mass grave of 73 mutilated victims buried in Love Lane Cemetery, 6 April.

THE FAVERSHAM 1916 EXPLOSION. The memorial erected over the mass grave of disaster victims. The history of gunpowder and explosives manufacture in the Faversham area includes a number of accidental explosions, involving varying numbers of casualties and degrees of damage. However, nothing had approached the severity of the 1916 detonation and its consequent loss of life which exceeded that of any previous such disaster in Britain.

FAVERSHAM WELCOMED THE RETURN OF CAPTAIN PHILIP NEAME, Royal Engineers, on 17 July 1915. Captain Neame had been awarded the Victoria Cross, and this picture of the wet day in summer shows Captian Neame's parents, officers, the mayor, mace-bearer and other dignitaries on the dais before the Guild Hall, facing a parade of military and fire brigade personnel. Lord Harris welcomed and congratulated the 26 year-old Captain Neame who was the son of Mr and Mrs Frederick Neame, formerly of Macknade. The guard of honour was provided by the 3rd West Lancs. RFA who were stationed locally. Captain Neame was afterwards entertained by the Mayor and Mayoress at Gatefield House in Preston Street. The large poster above the door of the Guild Hall is not completely readable but supports the war effort in referring to 'Filling the Ranks' and munitions.

Bottom right.
PEACE CELEBRATIONS 1919, the procession passing down Preston Street. Many shops and businesses provided entries. The precise point of this photograph may be determined by the well-known clock extending from a building on the right and, behind the horse-drawn float, the Fleur de Lis and the large tree in front of Gatefield House (now Alexander Centre) (see page 123 bottom).

IN A CLOSE-UP of the occasion shown on the facing page, Captain Neame is flanked by a senior officer and the mayor as he salutes the parade from the raised platform before the Guild Hall at this civic welcome. Newspaper reports of the time reported that at Neuve Chapelle in France, Captain Neame had stoutly resisted the German fire and grenades which had been decimating a section of British troops. He had also succeeded in rescuing a great number of wounded. On Monday the 19 July 1915, Captain Neame was at Windsor Castle where he was presented with his Victoria Cross medal by King George V.

COURT STREET. After the armistice in November 1918 a memorial service was held at Faversham on 3 August 1919 to mark the outbreak of the war five years earlier. A cenotaph was erected in Court Street where Crescent Road is now situated and the photograph shows a large crowd waiting in the hot August sunshine for the arrival of the procession which included army and naval units. The small, one-storey pedimented building, roughly centre of the picture, still exists and was built in 1810, originally to house the manually-operated town fire engine.

EVENTS TO MARK THE OUTBREAK AND CESSATION OF THE FIRST WORLD WAR were supported by large crowds in the years following the war. On 30 July 1919, a military tank – developed from the type which had appeared on the Flanders Front with such impact in 1916, although its potential was unrecognized by the Allied command of the time – was presented to the town of Faversham. Such items were generally used as memorials (cf. Ashford), but the ultimate fate of the Faversham example is uncertain. A few days after the arrival of the tank a memorial service was held in the town to mark the outbreak of the war (see facing page).

PEACE DAY on 19 July 1919 was celebrated in Faversham style. At the Recreation Ground Mr Hargrave was on hand as was usual on such occasions. He was able to capture this photograph of Maud Butler (later to become Mrs Queen) beautifully attired with her stunningly decorated pram and doll (see page 121 bottom).

A TURN OUT OF THE FIRE BRIGADE always occasioned excitement and the arrival of many onlookers. This scene in Abbey Street, undated but probably in the late 1920s after the acquisition of a motorised fire appliance, took place opposite the Phoenix Tavern (see page 144 top) on the right and outside the King's Head. The latter had previously offered hospitality under the name of The Mermaid, and subsequently The Smack. Although the pub no longer exists the alley hard by is still called Smack Alley. In the distance can be seen the jettied gable of Arden's House.

Bottom right.
FAVERSHAM CARNIVAL is a well-supported event of long standing. The 'Jolly Huntsman', complete with inn sign, was the float entered in around 1935 by T.A. Whittle & Co. With Arthur Butler at the window, the float was also manned by Charlie Benefield, Jack Downs, Albert Bottle, Sid Queen and 'Ponto' Harris. The bucolic scene was enhanced with genuine accessories such as the pewter mugs and long clay pipes.

A DINNER PARTY was held in early 1933 at The Ship Hotel for employees of the timber firm of T.A. Whittle & Co. In that year Mr Macey, a worker at the firm, had won £30,000 on an Irish sweepstake ticket and he provided the dinner to celebrate the event. These details were recalled by Mr Arthur Butler who is seated in the second row from the back, third from the right. In the same row can be seen Mr Macey next to Mr Davy who was wearing spectacles. Others included in the photograph were Mr S. Chambers, Mr Richards, Mr Stuart Chambers, Mr Les Queen, Mr Fred Owen and Mr Fred Branchett.

THE FONDNESS FOR PROCESSIONS is typified here by children taking part in the Faversham Co-operative Society's Gala Day on 16 August 1919. The parade is passing along Athelstan Road from Forbes Road where an open bank may be seen where bungalows now exist. In the distance to the left of the tree on the horizon, Delbridge House is silhouetted. Athelstan Road itself was built following the Forbes Road construction and railway station enlargement (see page 76).

THE FLOODS OF FEBRUARY 1953 overran the marshes and this view of the breached railway line near Graveney/Seasalter is annotated 'The biggest hole of the lot'. The scale of the floods prompted extensive sea-defence works along the Thames estuary and much of the local marshland was embanked and drained.

FAVERSHAM INSTITUTE stood in East Street where John Anderson Court now stands (see page 28 top). The old Institute hosted many local events and the example pictured here around 1929/30 shows The Scouts 3rd Faversham Pack using it for their jamboree. Here on stage Arthur Butler presided with the stick as he and others gave the Scouts' salute. Also present were boys named Sales, Tambling, Sayers, Cleaver and the two brothers Tambling.

A PLATOON OF THE HOME GUARD formed in Faversham in the Second World War. From the back: Stan Hurrall, George Low, Sid Huxted, Bert Gurr, Alan Baker, Alan White, Jim Allen, Charlie Luckhurst, George Vidler, Arthur Downes, Tommy Linkin, Percy Raines. They formed the Transport Section of the Home Guard and were drawn from the East Kent and Maidstone & District bus companies (see page 79).

SECTION SIX

Local Government, Schools and Services

MEMBERS OF THE BOROUGH OF FAVERSHAM on 20 September 1945, on the occasion of the admission of Councillor Phil Johnson, OBE, JP, Mayor, to the Honorary Freedom of the Borough. (The slightly whimsical manner of describing many of the officials has been retained as printed on the original photograph.) Back row: Mr C. Walton (The Sewage Works Manager), Councillor C.E. Ely, Mr G.A.J. McKinley (The Fire Guard Officer), Councillor T. Williams, Mr G.S. Sommerville (The Electrical Engineer), Councillor G.H. Tory, Mr H.G. Farndon (The Air Raid Precautions Officer), Councillor W.B. Holmes, Councillor The Revd M.E. Lynch, Mr G. Hulse (The Sergeant-at-Mace), Mr G.G. Culmer (The Sanitary Inspector), Councillor H. Knowles, Dr W.F. Adams (The Medical Officer of Health), Councillor T.W. Herdman Porter, Mr A.E. Smith (The Borough Treasurer), Councillor F.G. Johnson, Councillor A.W. Hulkes, Councillor C.G. Fuller, Mr C.P. Curling (The Ambulance & Transport Officer), Mr S. Percy Andrews (The Planning Officer). Front row: Mr S. Wilson (The Town Clerk), Alderman C.S. Hawkes, JP, The Revd W.A.R. Ball, MA, RD (The Mayor's Chaplain), Councillor J.B. Neame, JP (The Deputy Mayor), Councillor Phil Johnson, OBE, JP (The Mayor), Alderman J.W. Videan, JP, Alderman W.I. Gould, Alderman J.H. Johnson, JP, Mr A. Smith (The Clerk of the Peace).

SWALE RURAL DISTRICT COUNCIL on 27 February 1946. Back row (left to right): Capt. J.E. Prentis (Newnham), Mr C.C. Bishop (Upchurch), Capt. G.D. James (Throwley), Mr J.C. Harlow (Newington), Mr A.J. Meeson (Eastling), Mr A.L. Baker (Bapchild), Mr P. Lintott (Stalisfield), Mr T.M. Scutt (Badlesmere & Leaveland), Mr E.L. Coles (Bredgar), Mr D.J. Moor (Teynham). Second row: Mr W.S. Thomas (Lynsted), Mr G.E. Mannering (Halstow Lower), Mr L.A. Randerson (Engineer & Surveyor), Mr W.A. Dennett (Chief Financial Officer), Mr R.K. Dunning (Chief Sanitary Inspector), Mr Guy Tassell (Clerk of the Council), Mr Bryan Tassell (Deputy Clerk of the Council), Mr T.G. Churchill (Rent & Rate Collector), Mr H.H. Kitchener (Second Assistant Clerk), Revd W.J.B. Crouch (Borden), Mr J.M. Minter (Faversham Without, Goodnestone & Graveney), Mr A. Bones (Hernhill), Mr S. Stevens (Luddenham). Front row: Mr R.B. Amos (Sheldwich), Dr P. Selby (Acting Medical Officer of Health), Lt.-Col. G.E. Stevens (Bobbing & Iwade), Mr F. Ivo Neame (Chairman; Selling), Mr W.S. Stevens (Vice-Chairman; Hartlip), Mr. G. Sargent (Doddington), Mr W.H. Wilson (Boughton), Mr G.L. Heathfield (Oare), Capt. C.W.G.H. Wheler (Ospringe), Mr W.A. French (Buckland, Norton & Stone).

HENRY WREIGHT'S SCHOOL CONCERT PARTY at Christmas 1917 bringing some gaiety to a town that must have been feeling, in common with the rest of the country, a certain sense of sombreness in that particularly harrowing year of the First World War. More properly known as the Commercial School when built in 1857 in Church Road, with money drawn from Henry Wreight's benefaction to the town in 1840, the school became merged with Faversham Grammar School three years after this photograph was taken.

CAPTIONED 'THE GRAMMAR SCHOOL, BIG SCHOOLROOM', this photograph of post-1920 shows the fine hammer-beam roof construction of the main part of the Wreight School referred to in the above caption. The building has been restored under the sponsorship of Swale Borough Council and renamed 'Flint House'. This room is now used for community purposes and meetings, thus providing continuity with the past and welcome facilities for public use.

'FAVERSHAM GRAMMAR SCHOOL' is the caption to this photograph, showing the art room equipped with folding desks and natural history exhibits, including birds and animals in glass cases. It is in fact part of the original Wreight School referred to in the previous two illustrations, subsequent to the merger with the grammar school.

THESE SCHOOL BUILDINGS in Church Road survive due to their conversion to private dwellings. This fine photograph, probably taken in the early 1930s, shows the range in its earlier use when it was still a school. It was built as a new 'District National School' in 1852/3 with money from the Henry Wreight benefaction. The architect was R.C. Hussey who included a gatehouse and inner court in the design which proved admirably suitable for the recent adaptation to residential use.

FAVERSHAM DISTRICT NATIONAL SCHOOLS CLASS FIVE, probably 1907. The rear form on which the children are standing was rather precariously supported on wooden soap boxes, the contents of which, in the form of hard bars of soap, perhaps contributed to the freshly scrubbed appearance of the youngsters. The group are posed outside their flint and stone school built in Church Road, in 1853. The building has now been converted to private residential use and re-named St Mary's Court.

AT THE FAVERSHAM DISTRICT SCHOOL, CHURCH ROAD, on 10 July 1924, the girls were costumed and organized to play 'living whist', a somewhat complicated procedure liable to a certain confusion. The girls shown here include Lucy Wickins, Grace Cornelius, Dolly Beer, Ivy Holdstock, Hilda King, 'Midge' Wilkinson, Win Owen, Evelyn Jacobs, Connie Becket, Ella Ratcliffe, Eileen Honey, Flo Cornelius, Ivy King, Margaret Hackett and Elsie Manson.

THE ELIZABETHAN GRAMMAR SCHOOL, seen here in 1903, was built in the late sixteenth century as the result of eventual re-endowment following the demise of the original grammar school upon the dissolution of the abbey. It survives in the ownership of a Masonic society and is happily open to public inspection on some occasions during the year. At these times the first-floor schoolroom complete with desks and names carved thereon may be wondered at, and conjecture made about this tangible link with those times when Shakespeare and the unknown author of the 'Arden of Feversham' play knew the town.

THE COTTAGE HOSPITAL in Stone Street was built in 1887 on the site of worked out brickfields and thus stands on a much lower footing than the road at the original ground level. There have been various extensions to the hospital, the latest being opened for use in 1988, with the official opening by the Duke and Duchess of Kent on 31 January 1989. The new wing has been built in sympathetic style and is contiguous with the original buiding to the left of this picture utilizing the site of a former nonconformist church.

THE POLICE STATION built in 1904 in Church Road following the incorporation of the Faversham Police into the Kent Police in 1899. The members of the Force seen here appear to display a sense of pride in their building which was a great improvement on the old lock-up in Middle Row.

COPTON WINDMILL in around 1926. Basically a 'tower' mill constructed of brick, the main structure remains, but the cap was replaced by a water tank in c. 1930. The date at which the mill was first built is a little uncertain but it was probably in around 1870, its purpose being to raise water for the Faversham Water Company. Even the water tank crowning the top has gone now and the tower, of listed building status, stands embarrassed, empty and forced to gaze upon the motorway traffic.

SECTION SEVEN

Breweries, Pubs and Shops

A. HUGHES' BUTCHER'S SHOP, Westgate Road, *c.* 1870. Mr Hughes is here seen standing outside his shop which has the kind of open display of meat and carcases once common at such establishments. As here, a variety of game was usually on offer in addition to domestically-reared meat.

THE ROAD THROUGH GRAVENEY leads to The Sportsman public house at the western end of Seasalter and near the point marking the beginning of South Swale Nature Reserve, which stretches along the shore line to the mouth of Faversham Creek on the Swale. The Sportsman remains a popular rendezvous for walkers and holiday visitors, just as it was in the early 1900s when this photograph was taken showing various early means of transport as well as a tantalizing glimpse of some outdoor activity in progress. The enormous empty barrels are witness to the attractions of the house for tired travellers.

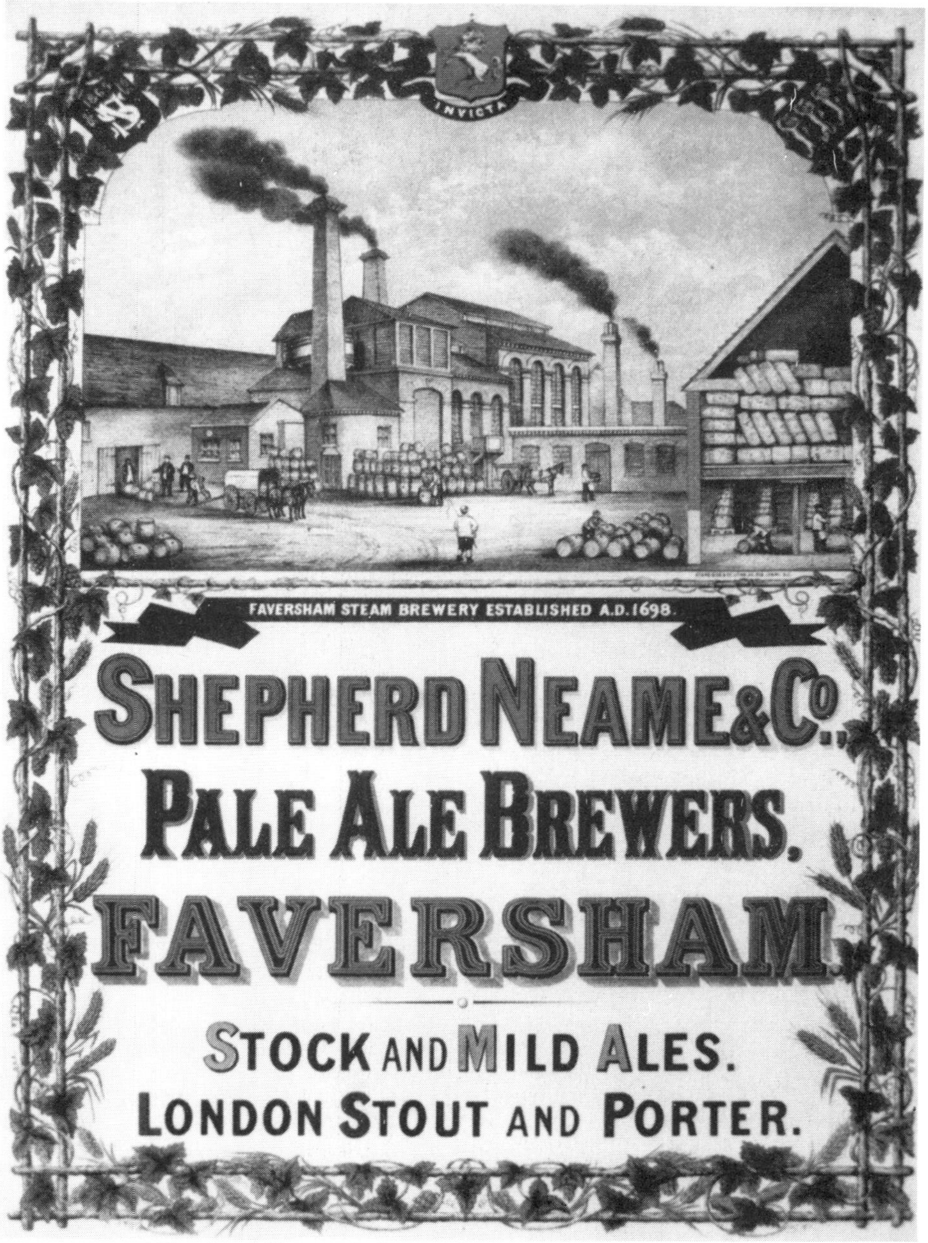

THE BREWERY of Shepherd Neame & Co was founded in 1698 by Richard Marsh who later became Town Mayor. The 1865 lithograph reproduced here, was a colourful poster partly depicting the Shepherd Neame 'steam brewery' as it then appeared.

THE PRESENT APPEARANCE OF SHEPHERD NEAME OFFICES at 16/17 Court Street suggests a single symmetrical building erected in Victorian decorative style with hop-bine moulding embellishing the sides of the main entrance. In 1869 when built, the office building appeared as in this illustration. It was not until 1900 that the shop at number 16 was demolished and the left-hand side of the present offices were added in matching style to the existing number 17.

OUTSIDE THE SHEPHERD NEAME OLD BOTTLING STORE in 1947, Charlie 'Polly' Sinden was pictured beside his delivery vehicle in the Conduit Street area.

OSPRINGE, MAISON DIEU AND WATER LANE. This photograph, probably taken *c.* 1930, shows the use to which the building was put in 1895 when the shop windows were inserted. This part of Maison Dieu is now in the care of the Ministry of the Environment. It is part of the original foundation of 1230 that provided hospitality and shelter for Canterbury pilgrims, and was part of the complex that extended on the north side of the main road, where accommodation was available for the use of royalty when *en route* to the Continent.

SHIPWRIGHTS ARMS, Hollow Shore *c.* 1895. At the confluence of Faversham and Oare creeks stands the Shipwrights Arms, an old inn more comfortably approached by boat than by car, although many choose the latter method and find the effort well worthwhile. The inn sits low behind the sea wall and more than once in its life it has been inundated by floods. However, it shrugs off such irrelevancies and continues to provide welcome refreshment for customers arriving by land and water (see page 38 top).

THE GREYHOUND in Partidge Lane with Henry Page affirming, by a notice above his bar window, his right to sell beer for consumption on the premises. From an upstairs window a lady peeps at the photographer from behind the open sash. The Greyhound closed in 1960, and after a period of use as a private residence it was demolished in 1970. As late as 1926 when this photograph was taken, the black dog on the right of the picture could still pursue that acme of doggy heaven – lying in the middle of a dusty road on a hot day.

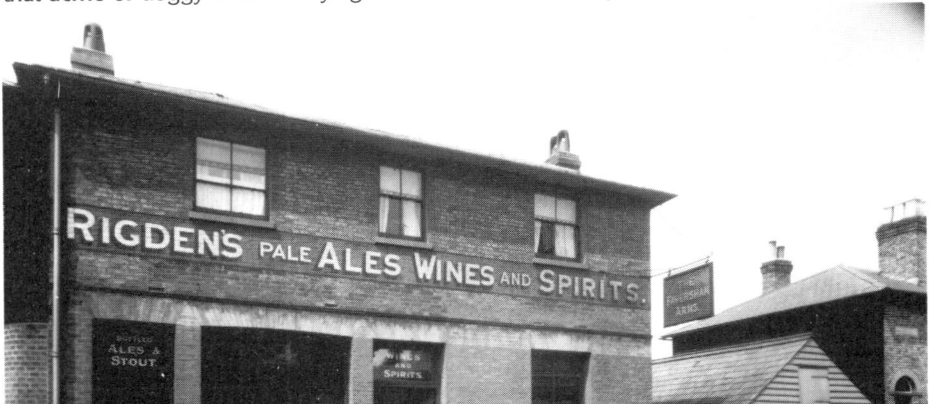

IN OSPRINGE ROAD the nineteenth-century pub The Faversham Arms, had George Sergeant as landlord in 1926 when this photograph was taken. The building had been erected in around 1850 on part of the land formerly known as Hangman's Field, and later as Gallow's Hole Field, from the one-time situation of the town gallows there. On the wall of the garage to the right a South-East and Chatham Railway advertisement features the Cannon Street Hotel in London.

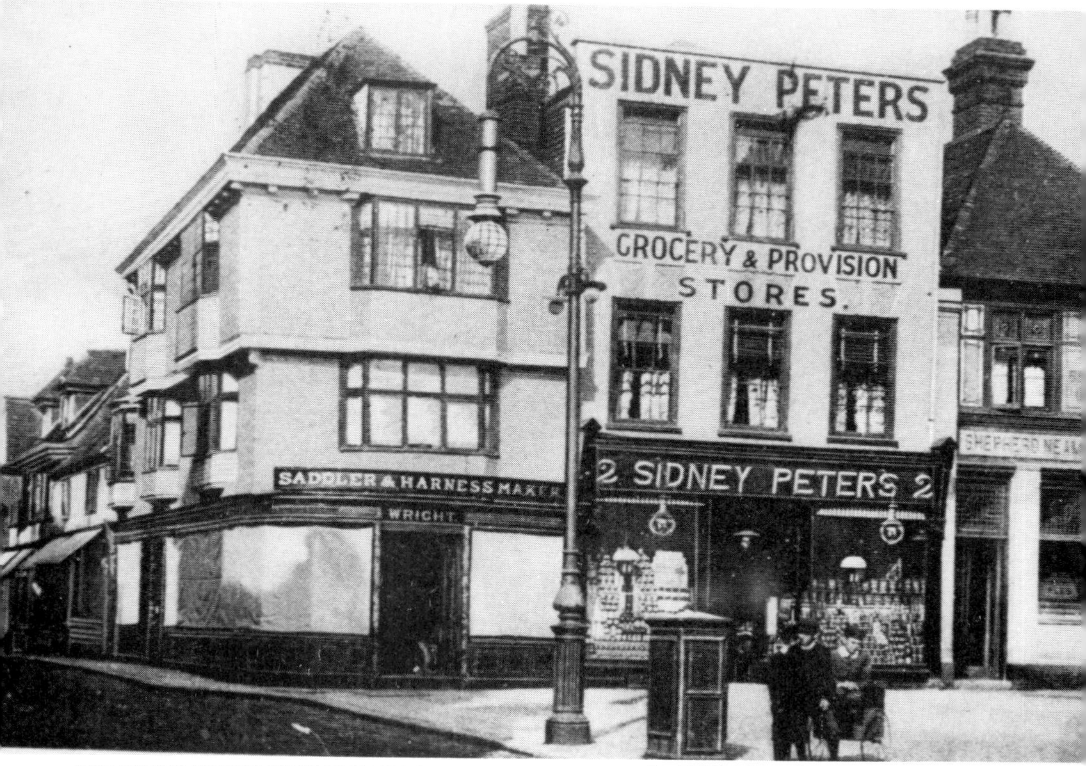

ONE OF THE BEST-KNOWN CORNERS OF FAVERSHAM, as seen in 1908. West Street with its many medieval buildings leads down the hill to the left. The corner three-storeyed timber-framed building with jettied upper floor was occupied by Wright's saddlery and harness shop. Sidney Peters' 'Grocery and Provision Stores' was formerly the post office, and next to that, partly concealed by the corner of the Guildhall, is Shepherd Neame's The Bear Inn. The proud owners of the small handcart fitted with old pram wheels stand near one of the town's first electric lamp-standards.

THE PHOENIX TAVERN in Abbey Street displayed a proud claim to 'Kent's Best' in 1926, under the newly formed company name of George Beer and Rigden following the acquisition of Rigden's brewery by George Beer of Canterbury. The building absorbs the remains of a fourteenth-century hall within the present fabric.

AT THE WESTERN END OF THE VILLAGE OF NEWNHAM The Royal Oak, retailing Rigden's beers, provided competition to The George in the early 1900s, but after the First World War it reverted to private residential use. Bert Forster (see page 55) was licensee here for a time, and the building, which is probably early nineteenth-century in date, is now known as Audrey House.

THE DOLPHIN HOTEL, Preston Street, in the 1930s after alterations to the Victorian façade. This entailed the addition of glazed tiling on the ground floor with some modification of the windows at this level also. Where there had been formerly a three-light window this was now reduced to two lights filling the same overall width, but interestingly the Victorian moulded mullion had been saved and reused. All to little avail though, together with the timber-framed premises on the left, so long occupied by the photographer T.U. Barber, it has become a casualty of questionable (to say the least) development.

THE STAR INN in Middle Row now forms part of an extensive development providing warden-assisted private accommodation for people over the age of 55. The Star dates from around 1600 when it was called The Chequers, later becoming The Gun and finally acquiring the name seen here some time after John Rigden bought the property from Charlotte Corne for £260 in 1785. In 1926 the billposters on the adjacent wall advertised amusements including a carousel, 'flying chair-o-planes', and a 'grand violin orchestra-phone'. Also advertised was the auction of a block of five freehold dwelling houses and a shop in West Street (numbers 34–38 inclusive) which were producing a combined rent of £91 17*s*. 4*d*. per annum.

THE BULL INN at the corner of West Street and Tanners Street stands where the medieval centre of the town is thought to have originated. The building certainly pre-dates 1600 and was recorded in this photograph in 1926, when not all of Rigden's signs had been changed to include George Beer's name also.

BOUGHTON. The Ship Inn in this photograph appears to have had a steep slope leading to even steeper steps up to the front door. No doubt there were occasions that this approach must have posed difficulties for some customers leaving the inn. The added buildings which can be seen here on the end of the pub have now mostly been removed and the former hostelry is a private house. This range of buildings is now most attractive with one nearer the far end having exposed timber framework.

IN PRESTON STREET the present Hole in The Wall pub was formerly known as the Albion Wine Vaults with deeds going back to 1619. A description of 1664 included 'malthouses' and in 1770 over an acre of hop garden was included in the sale of the property to Valentine Court. It was acquired by Rigdens in 1912 from the Court family who had retained ownership previously. This 1926 photograph has many interesting details such as various wines and spirits offered for sale at prices ranging from 3*s*. 6*d*. (17½p) to 10*s*. (50p) a bottle. If you felt that restraint was called for, an adjacent shop window reveals that you may have obtained corsets for 2*s*. 11*d*.

EDWARDIAN PRESTON STREET with many young people among the shoppers. The windows of the Home and Colonial grocery stores, and A. M. Edwards, stationer and bookseller, were full of wares. On the left can be seen the large tree that grew in front of Gatefield House (now Council Offices) a little beyond the Fleur de Lis which is now the Faversham Heritage Centre. Many buildings can be identified, although one of the oldest, Knowles the fruiterers, fell foul of British Gas showroom development in 1965, only to be spurned and vacated by them a few years ago.

THE FOUR HORSE SHOES AT GRAVENEY with empty barrels outside awaiting return to the brewery in 1926. At this time the whole of the pub name, brewer etc, was painted on the brickwork of the building. The only separate sign proclaimed 'You may phone from here'. There are many oil stains outside but the road surface indicates that motoring was still a dusty business in dry weather.

SECTION EIGHT

Sport and Leisure

FAVERSHAM RECREATION GROUND with a cricket match in progress. In the distance is the gardener's lodge erected after the park site was purchased in 1860. In front of that can be seen the bandstand of 1895 which survived until the last war. The children in the foreground evidently found Mr Filmer's performance as photographer of more interest than that of the cricketers.

AT THE HIGHER END OF THE RECREATION GROUND there is situated the gardener's cottage built after the 20-acre site was bought in 1860 largely with money from the charity set up from Henry Wreight's bequest to the town. The bandstand was donated later by Alderman Child in 1895 but unhappily met its demise in the Second World War, although only indirectly by enemy action – it was scrapped for the war effort. Long before that unfortunate official and necessary vandalism took place, this photograph was taken. Its detail reveals the extent and intricacy of the late Victorian ironwork.

THE SERIOUS NATURE OF FOOTBALL in 1907 is confirmed by this picture of the 1st Kent RA Volunteers, Faversham No. 3 Co. XI, who won the regimental cup in that year. A point of interest is the different nature of football boots at that time; thick leather and laced well over the ankles they appear less flexible than those used today. They would also have made shin pads an essential aid to self-preservation.

THE MANUFACTURE OF EXPLOSIVES AT THE OARE FACTORY, where some decaying evidence of the industry survives, was in the hands of Curtis & Harvey Ltd. for the first quarter of this century, before it passed to ICI for a few more years until closure in 1934. Social and sporting activities were popular and encouraged; here the opposing teams posed for a group picture in 1908 when a match took place at Faversham between the local Curtis & Harvey works and the London office.

THE COTTON POWDER COMPANY had its own rifle club which held a match on 21 November 1908 between married and single members. The members are pictured here at their firing position. In the background are some of the company's buildings which were widely-spaced apart in order to lessen the effect of accidental explosions.

PUB OUTINGS were a popular feature in the two-brewery town of Faversham, and in 1924, The Bear outing, which started from opposite the establishment in Market Place, required two Daimler motor coaches. A study of the participants' faces leaves no doubt that this was an affair of the utmost seriousness.

THE SPORT OF GOALRUNNING was popular in the district with clubs at Faversham, Throwley, Teynham, Whitstable, Oare and Ospringe. Faversham Athletic Goalrunning Club were District Champions in 1920 and were pictured here in the following year. League matches were played with as many as thirty bare-footed players per side. For about three-quarters of an hour the game was one of frantic activity with players taking turns to sprint from home base and back after passing their flag. Players from the opposing team would do likewise with points being scored for a 'stroke', i.e., touching an opponent. This was apparently a Kentish game of two or three hundred years standing. It has now died out supposedly in favour of football, or perhaps the energy demanded for the sport is beyond the inclinations of many today.

Bottom right.
A SECOND FAVERSHAM RINK-HOCKEY TEAM in 1920 was also managed by Mr Ellis (centre back). Known as 'The Rink Hockey Club', the group pictured here also includes Jim West (standing far left), Bob Macey (seated far left) and Bob Peake the goalkeeper. A Faversham team became famous in 1930, representing Great Britain in an international competition at Montreux where they became champions.

THE FAVERSHAM 'FIVERS' HOCKEY CLUB TEAM in 1920 when they won the Rose Bowl Competition. Mr Ellis, the manager, is the centre standing figure and the left-hand seated player is known to have been named Day. The form of hockey played was 'rink' hockey, the players wearing roller skates as can be clearly seen in this picture. The skating rink was in a converted building near the head of Faversham Creek. The building was destroyed by fire in 1925 and facilities at Herne Bay were used for some years.

CHARABANC OUTINGS were not the prerogative of pubs. The Faversham Wesleyan Church choir gathered for their trip to Hastings on 5 July 1928. Such photographs were invariably posed in good weather, but on wet occasions the transport available (despite the folding hood) must have demanded a certain stoicism and determination to enjoy oneself, come what may. The coach appears to have been provided by the Maidstone and District Coach Co.

FIELD SPORTS were a popular recreation for men who generally worked longer hours than are common today. Football had many devotees and a fair proportion of valuable spare time was given up to the pursuit of this serious competitive sport. This photograph of Faversham Amateurs FC in 1905–6 is particularly interesting in showing the names of the players. Back row, left to right: Mathews, Turner, Foley, H. Ellis, Marsh, Shrubsall, Balcombe, Redman, A. Day, Luck, Rowlands, A. Ellis, Swan.

SHELDWICH FOOTBALL CLUB 1922–23 season. Left to right: Alick Checksfield, Herbert Kendrick, D. Gould, –?–, Viv Stokes, –?–, ? Evans, ? Austin, –?–, H. Checksfield, –?–, –?–, Fred Checksfield. The family likeness of the three Checksfield players can be discerned quite clearly in the photograph.

ACKNOWLEDGEMENTS

The willing help and interest of many people have made possible the production of this book. I have frequently enlisted the aid of others whose knowledge and recollections of Faversham and district far exceed my own, and in such cases their assistance has been invaluable and given unstintingly. To lend old family photographs for a period of months could cause some misgivings on the part of the owners. For their patience and trust I am deeply grateful and with sincere appreciation I acknowledge the generosity and assistance of the following:

Mr Max Ardley • Mr & Mrs A. Butler • Mr & Mrs C. Clark • Mrs L. Hodges
Mr Graham Jones • Mr & Mrs M. Mesher • Mr Peter Morgan • Mr Michael Peters
Mrs L. Richards • Mr & Mrs D. Raines • Mrs Audrey Swain • Mr Antony Swain
Miss Pam Wright • Mrs B. Rogers, Hon. Curator, The Fleur de Lis Heritage Centre
Mr B. Mulhern, Advertising & Promotions Manager, Messrs. Shepherd Neame Ltd
Mr N. Redman, Archivist and Mr Arthur Willis, Packaging & Warehouse Manager, Messrs Whitbread & Co. PLC.

To all others who have assisted me in any way, my thanks are duly recorded also.